Maggie Tisserand runs the successful company *Matisse Aromatherapy* which exports essential oils to Japan. Well known in Japan, she has a range of natural toiletries bearing her name, as well as being the leader in the aromatherapy oil market. Her work involves a great deal of travel to source new products for the Japanese market as well as for her Brighton-based aromatherapy mail order business. She also lectures on the benefits of aromatherapy both in the UK and abroad.

Maggie has three children and currently lives in Sussex.

STRESS: The Aromatic Solution

Maggie Tisserand

In collaboration with

Dr. Peter Helps, M.B., BSc, AC, MRTCM

Hodder & Stoughton

First published in 1996
by Hodder and Stoughton
A division of Hodder Headline PLC

Copyright © 1995 by Maggie Tisserand
Illustrations © Rodney Paul

10 9 8 7 6 5 4 3 2 1

British Library Cataloguing in Publication Data
Tisserand, Maggie
Stress: Aromatic Solution
I. Title
155.9042

ISBN 0 340 64902 X

Typeset by Hewer Text Composition Services, Edinburgh
Printed and bound in Great Britain by
Cox and Wyman Ltd, Reading

Hodder and Stoughton Ltd
A Division of Hodder Headline PLC
338 Euston Road
London NW1 3BH

This book is dedicated to the doctor within

ACKNOWLEDGEMENTS

My grateful thanks go to the following people, all of whom have been an important part in the creation of this book.

To the nurses of the Royal Sussex County Hospital who took part in, and brought so much positive feedback to, the Nurses Stress Project. And to the NHS Trust personnel who not only gave me the go ahead, but donated much valuable input and practical help with the setting up of the Project. To Leda McFarlene, Jill Dunley and all of the massage therapists from the Wilbury Training Centre who so generously gave of their time and energies. To my son James and to Poraig for his computer wizardry which enabled usable data to be collated from the hundreds of questionnaires completed during the Project.

To Peter Helps MB, BSc, AC, MRTCM for his contribution to Chapters 1 and 2 and for his time in overseeing the medical aspects of the book.

To Elisabeth Millar for her enthusiasm and practical help at the conceptual and early stages of writing this book, and to Julie Corbin for her support and ever willing assistance in bringing this book to completion.

To all of the Sussex practitioners who have generously given information for Chapter 6:– Richard Davison, MRCST; Ruth Urbanowicz BSc, MMCA; Gareth Francis BA (Hons), Dip NLP; Sue Tomkins MIFR; Hanna Waldbaum LCH; Vincent Tilsley MA (Oxon), Dip HP, MNAHP; Marek Urbanowicz MAc, MTAcS; Sarah Bristow MRSS; Roberta Morgan, Dip ION. An extra thank you to Roberta Morgan for her nutritional expertise without which Chapter 4 would not exist in its current form.

To Sarah Ardern for her stress-releasing 'foot hold' described in the Illustrated Techniques of Application, and for her expertise in helping to release my stress during the final months of writing and to Betty Hutchings for her unfailing support and advice. To my two daughters, Lucy and Saffron, for feeding me and my cats whilst I battled with publishing deadlines. And to Mike for his love and patience.

MEDICAL DISCLAIMER

This book is not intended as a substitute for professional help. If your symptoms persist you should consult a qualified practitioner.

CONTENTS

INTRODUCTION

Is stress really on the increase or are we just more aware of it at present? Certainly stress is receiving a lot of newspaper column inches at the current time. Recent headlines have run, variously – 'When the stress of your job can show in your face', 'How tension takes its toll on your body', 'Strain of the office tells on the modern man . . .' And if you thought that stress was solely confined to the general public, you would be entirely wrong. 'Doctors in distress' is an article about GPs who are unable to cope with the demands of their job. Paramedics, armed forces personnel, nursing staff, hospital doctors, police, teachers – all are finding the stress of their jobs increasing to danger levels, with escalating rates of illness, depression, insomnia and a whole host of other stress-related diseases.

This doesn't augur well for the average person, who, for generations, has looked to the professionals for help in times of need. When we visit our doctor to discuss our stressful life and seek his opinion and help, we could be talking to someone who is finding it difficult to cope with their own stress. Stress knows no boundaries, and its effects can be equally devastating to the person living on the breadline as to the well-paid and comfortably off person. As far as stress is concerned, we are all equal.

However, we *do* have a choice in how stress progresses. The progression is all too often from Stress to Distress or from Dis-Ease to Disease. But by using techniques found in this book, the shift can easily be from Stress to De-Stress.

In the UK we have the benefit of a National Health

Service with free diagnosis, free drugs, free surgery.
We may have been brought up to believe 'doctor knows
best' and so for every stress-induced complaint we
experience, we can try a variety of pills to take the
problem away. For insomnia – sleeping tablets (down-
ers); for depression – benzodiazapenes such as valium
(uppers); for an upset stomach – antacids; for recurrent
chest infections – antibiotics; for back pain – NSAIDs
(non-steroidal anti-inflammatory drugs) such as para-
cetamol. Each of these drugs has been created to deal
with one specific symptom. Yet each of these symptoms
is only an outward sign of an inner stress.

But what happens when we take the drugs? The
immune system works less efficiently which increases
the likelihood of requiring another drug. And so the
pattern continues. A downhill slide all the way for our
health, but an upward trend for the drug company
profits. Who is the winner and who is the loser? Most
certainly it is our health and well-being that is the
loser. Because our body is losing its powers of self-
healing and we are handing over responsibility for our
health to an outside force – doctor, pharmacist, hospital surgeon.

For those who are under stress, and just beginning to
notice things going wrong – be it an inability to sleep,
irritability, forgetfulness, neck ache, recurring headaches, indigestion – whatever the problem, it should be
addressed now, gently and efficiently, with aromatherapy and allied alternative therapies, before it grows
into a big problem that can only be treated with more
conventional methods. Once you have reached 'the
point of no return' – when your body has become
accustomed to medication to keep it functioning –
then it is vital that the drugs are continued, for to
stop suddenly could be fatal. But why wait for things to
go wrong in your body – take responsibility for your
health. Be an active participant in your own health,
find your own power and know that you *can* make a
difference.

Stress is an all too frequent bedfellow for the busy
person, including me, and I am indebted to aromatherapy for enabling me to let go of, and rise above, every

stressful encounter. Aromatherapy is particularly good for releasing both mental and physical tension and bringing about a feeling of peace and tranquillity. Often the transformation begins to work the moment that the essential oil, or blend of essential oils, is inhaled. What this means is that after just one massage or aromatic bath, you will almost certainly feel that you have taken the first step on the road to recovery, and that your particular stress-induced problem can be easily and successfully addressed. The aim of this book is to illustrate how many of our current ailments are directly linked to stress, and how, with the judicious use of essential oils, it becomes a simple pleasure to rectify the harm done by our stressful lifestyle.

1

What Is Stress?

Stress is something that we all experience, irrespective of gender, age, financial situation, marital status or geographical location. There is no natural immunity to stress – it is a part of everyday living. The most happy, carefree child of five, if momentarily separated from its mother whilst out shopping, will experience stress. The mother may have been contentedly choosing vegetables for the evening meal, but on realising that her child is missing she will become acutely stressed and remain in that state until she is reunited with her child. This is nature; this is natural. Stress is with us from the cradle to the grave. Acute stress gives us the alertness and strength to search all day and all night, if necessary, without the need to fulfil any of the normal bodily functions of eating, defecating or sleeping, until the child is safely restored to us. In such a context, stress is not harmful. We are being given extra resources to cope with an emergency situation, and as soon as the trauma is over – whether it has lasted for a matter of minutes or for several hours – the body will readjust and life will carry on as normal.

The noun 'stress', used in any context, always implies an accentuation, an emphasis, a force. According to the Oxford Dictionary, one definition of stress is 'a pressure of load, weight, some adverse force or influence, etc'; and in a paperback thesaurus one selection of words which can be substituted for the word 'stress' reads: 'anxiety, burden, hassle, nervous tension, oppression, pressure, strain, tautness, tension, trauma, worry'.

Each of these words could be applied to the person who is finding it difficult to cope with the complexities of living in the lead-up to the twenty-first century, and we are now beginning to recognise that stress is the major health issue in industrialised societies. Let's look at some of the forms in which it typically appears: the stress of holding down a job in a climate of increasing unemployment; the stress involved with working from nine till five in a job which is over-demanding or unfulfilling, and possibly for a boss who is difficult to work for; repossession of the family home as the mortgage cannot be met; bringing up children in towns and cities which are becoming increasingly lawless and frightening; soaking up sadness and despondency from our daily newspapers and television programmes. This is not acute stress but chronic stress, and we could rightly claim to be 'suffering from stress'. A daily diet of stress causes a loss of well-being, a nagging dis-ease, and for many people a hopeless sense of being trapped in a hostile world. Our society makes many demands upon us throughout our lives and we have to face painful experiences. It is when our resources to meet these challenges are over-taxed that a state of stress can develop, and the implications for our health become far-reaching.

Stress may manifest itself in many different ways. Common patterns include musculo-skeletal aches and pains, tension in the muscles of the neck and back, headaches, irritability, anxiety, insomnia, poor concentration, palpitations, gastro-intestinal disorders, menstrual disturbance and low sex drive. The immune system may be compromised, leading to repeated infections, auto-immune disorders and an increased susceptibility to cancer.

One of the intriguing things about stress is that we sense it is not necessarily a bad thing. Both folklore and contemporary culture are full of tales of heroes who endure great trials and tribulations and emerge triumphant. We gain great inspiration from these legends, whose themes are remodelled in countless forms down the ages. We humans seem to like challenges, and young people in particular often enjoy dangerous sports and activities such as bungee-jumping which might easily be seen as stressful. Our physiology changes and adapts to challenges in the familiar 'fight or flight' reaction: increased heart rate and respiration, heightened arousal, increased muscle tone, sharpened perception; and when the challenge is over we get a great sense of wellbeing and a feeling of accomplishment. It seems that we can cope with stress in short bursts, with plenty of time for rest and recuperation. But when stress is prolonged and associated with hopelessness and helplessness, the physiological changes are damaging to our health.

Stress Is Not Being In Control

Taking a ride on a roller-coaster in a fairground or theme park is a popular leisure activity. Everyone experiences terror and real fear, but the ride only lasts a few minutes and the stress experienced is transient and quickly replaced by euphoria – you have survived! Now imagine that, instead of experiencing a carefully controlled fairground ride, you are driving your car down a steep hill when suddenly the brakes fail. You no longer have control over the car, even though you are still able to steer, listen to the cassette player, turn the heating up or down, open the windows and operate many of the other functions of your car. Without control of the car's brakes you are in danger of having a serious accident and you are going to experience intense stress, fear and panic. Unlike the roller-coaster situation, in which you knew it would only last for a short time and also that someone was in control, in your own brakeless car you are helpless to control the speed at which you are travelling.

Much of what happens in our world is beyond our control. We may not be able to find a satisfying job – or any job at all; we can't change our boss's personality; and short of moving to the country there is little we can do about the rising crime in our urban society. If our lives seem to be perpetually stressful it could be that we have lost control (or never actually had control) and we experience fear, or at least anxiety, on a semi-permanent basis. Chronic anxiety easily leads to depression, and the combination can wreck our health and wellbeing.

Same Stressor – Different Subject

Mental attitude to stress is a critical factor in the way in which each person deals with their situation. Is there a feeling of 'being a victim'? That there is nothing to be done to help the situation? And what other factors are in play? Many things have a bearing on our handling of stressful situations – our past experiences; the attitudes of our partner or children; whether or not we have a spiritual anchor; confidence in our own ability; a willingness to take on a challenge (which could be seen as taking a gamble); the strength to start from scratch if need be; openness and an ability to confide in someone else about the situation; being able to admit what has happened/is happening. All these and more shape our responses to stress, and just as it is impossible to compare our own pain levels with those of another person, it is similarly impossible to compare stress loads.

With regard to stress, never has a saying been more pertinent than 'One man's meat is another man's poison'. A given situation could affect two people in entirely different ways. Let's look at some examples: first, that of two mothers who each find that their teenage daughter is smoking marijuana at parties.

Meg used to smoke pot during the sixties and considers

herself a bit of an ex-hippie. She is naturally concerned that her daughter should continue to study and gain good grades at A-Level so that she can go on to further education. But she can't be too angry or upset, because her child is only doing what she herself has done, and to condemn the action would be hypocritical. So she talks to her daughter, explaining that the use of dope is illegal, that the odd party joint may well be tolerated, but if the school work starts to slide then a report will be made to the school and any consequences will have to be dealt with. The stressful situation has been defused.

Ella either smoked dope in the sixties and won't admit it, or never touched the stuff. She totally panics when she finds what her child has been doing, and is confrontational. The mother wants her daughter to achieve good grades at A-Level and go on to university and desperately tries to impose her will upon the teenager. The daughter reacts by asserting her own will and the two have continual head-on clashes. The mother becomes anxious, smokes, drinks and, feeling too ashamed to talk to anyone about 'her problem', suffers acute symptoms of stress which include insomnia, lack of appetite and tachycardia. She takes the situation personally and feels as though she has failed as a mother.

Here's another typical example. Redundancies in the workplace are an everyday occurrence, but for the people concerned it can have either a devastating or beneficial effect on their lives.

Roger, MD of a large company in London, is made redundant in his fifties. He has been used to commuting to work each day and has coped well with the stress of the job for many years. Immediately he starts to look for a job of comparable status and financial reward. He has no success and, getting a little depressed, decides to set up his own business working from home. He finds that his expertise is a saleable commodity and in his first year of business the turnover is greater than he had envisaged. He also finds that working from home is less stressful and that he has more time and energy to give to his family.

Eventually he is thankful for the opportunities that redundancy has provided.

Carl, at fifty, finds himself in the same situation after being a successful executive for more than thirty years. He too searches for a new position in a large company but is unsuccessful. He can't face the fact that he is unemployed and pretends to his wife and neighbours that he is still working. Every morning he catches the same train, but instead of going to the office he spends the day in libraries and cafés – he is living a lie. It isn't long before he becomes depressed, can't sleep at night and starts to drink more. His health – both mental and physical – deteriorates until he is asking his doctor for 'something to help me sleep', and 'something to make me feel better', and soon he becomes reliant on anti-depressants and tranquillisers. Ultimately he suffers from angina or has a heart attack, and blames it on his redundancy.

Finally, the divorce rate is regularly quoted as being as high as one in three couples, and consequently there are millions of single parents. But people respond to the situation in very different ways.

Twin sisters both married within months of each other whilst in their twenties, and then divorced within a year of each other in their mid-thirties. Each has a young family to support, a difficult separation/divorce arrangement and severe financial problems. But the way in which each deals with the situation influences their health, wellbeing and future happiness.

Angela decides to rebuild her life, doing her utmost for her children. She refuses to criticise their father in front of them as she wishes to protect them from any further distress. She feels obvious resentment towards her ex-husband but tries to forgive him in her heart and to wish him well. She takes care of her health, both mental and physical, and has respect for her body. She works hard to support herself and the children, but she takes the time to go for a massage or a walk in the country. Because she is willing to forgive and let go of past hurts and injustices, she feels good in herself and is able to show compassion to others. Eventually she meets a wonderful man, a little battle-scarred from his own first marriage, and begins a happy, loving and sexually fulfilling long-term relationship.

Mary is very bitter towards her ex-husband and constantly denigrates him to whoever will listen. As her children grow older they feel uncomfortable in her presence and spend increasingly longer periods of time with their father to avoid listening to their mother's negativity. She is so busy putting down her ex that she hasn't any time or energy to take care of herself. She becomes apathetic, consoles herself with food (chocolates, endless cups of tea with biscuits, cakes, sweet liqueurs) and puts on a lot of weight. Even years later she still feels resentful – and not just towards her ex-husband. She now resents the way she looks and feels but, although she is sometimes motivated to attend weight watching meetings, she doesn't believe that she can effect a change. She has victim mentality. In her forties she suffers from dysmenorrhoea, fibroids and bones that break easily. Eventually she is advised to have a hysterectomy, which she is happy to do as she has no confidence in herself and has completely lost interest in the opposite sex.

As Louis Pasteur used to say, 'it is not the germ that matters, it is the soil.' Although he was referring to the human ability to withstand disease from germs by having a strong constitution/immune system, the same analogy could be applied to stress. Instead of germs which cause disease we are seeing many stress-induced diseases, along with an increase in the numbers of diseases which take hold when the immune system is not working efficiently. So the 'healthy soil' referred to by Pasteur has to be our ability to maintain our health by becoming masters of our stress – to stay intact and not allow a negative reaction to the stressful life event to rob us of our health and happiness.

It is not the stressful situation, therefore, which is of prime importance in the equation; it is the state of the recipient which is critical. If the person is already under stress, and has struggled to cope with half a dozen minor difficulties in a short period of time, then problem number seven could be the one to overload the system. We could liken this to plugging several electrical items into an adaptor and plugging that into the mains. Under normal usage the electric current flows through each appliance, but if too many appliances require electricity all at once the result will be a blown fuse. It is the same with our ability to cope with stress.

Patrick is a professional man in his late forties. His workload means he has to put in long hours, five days a week. The work is tiring and repetitive and he has difficulty in dragging himself out of bed in the mornings to face the day ahead. He has a wife who nags him and who doesn't understand what he is putting himself through in order to support the family and home. His stress manifests as psoriasis.

Kevin, a young man with a mortgage, a wife and three young children to support, drives to work each day in the rush hour, hating every minute. He works all day for a boss he can't stand, in a job which doesn't motivate him. He feels trapped and would like to resign but fears the consequences of not having a job. His stress manifests as a stomach ulcer, insomnia and depression, for which he seeks medical help.

Ruth, in her eighties, has suffered from high blood pressure (for which she takes prescribed medication) for more years than she can remember. Since her teenage years, when she was sent away from home, she has bottled up her emotions and refuses to let herself cry. She never likes to upset people but, lacking assertiveness, finds herself under increasing stress because she finds it difficult to say no. Her 'internalised' stress has manifested as hypertension, and even thinking about her unhappy teenage years is enough to send her blood pressure soaring.

Lydia is a love-sick divorcee who waits in vain for the phone call that never comes. Normally she is an independent, resilient person who manages to stay healthy, even when coping with a very busy work schedule. A winter bout of influenza forces her to stay in bed for a few days and, whilst resting, she constantly thinks about the object of her desires. Sensing that her plight is that of 'unrequited love', she cries a lot over the hopelessness of her situation and becomes very depressed. She recovers from the flu, but doesn't recover her vitality and feels constantly tired, with aching leg muscles and an increased desire to sleep. Her energy levels are so low that even driving to the shops and back exhausts her, and she has to go to sleep for an hour in order to recoup enough energy to cook dinner. She is constantly tearful, exhausted and unenthusiastic. Eventually she visits her GP for advice, and is diagnosed as having post-viral syndrome – the precursor of ME.

Without realising it, our chosen occupation and the length of time spent doing it can be incredibly stressful. Sometimes we put ourselves through immense stresses, simply because we are over-confident in our ability to 'burn the candle at both ends'.

Consider the case of Paul, a computer programmer who was very enthusiastic about a new computer language. He worked as a 'contractor' for four days a week, sitting in front of a screen for seven hours per day. His enthusiasm was so great that he also taught the language to private students in the evenings, which meant that on some days he was sitting for ten hours or more in front of a computer screen.

Aside from computing he had other interests, and in order to fit everything in he conditioned himself to take no more than four hours' sleep a night – which he managed to achieve for some time. When he reduced his sleep levels to two hours per night he began to notice that he felt tired, and one day when driving on a motorway he was convinced that the steering on his car had gone wrong, because the vehicle kept listing towards the hard shoulder. It was only when he woke up in a pile of cones that he realised what he had done – he had been depriving himself of the sleep that his body needed and had fallen asleep whilst driving.

By way of compensating for his chronic lack of sleep, he decided to spend the weekend sleeping for as long as his body dictated – which amounted to just over eighteen hours. Shortly after he woke up he went to his car, lifted out a box of envelopes and, on attempting to stand upright, experienced more pain than he had ever known before. His muscles had relaxed to such an extent that they were not able to support him, and his back just 'went'. Weeks of osteopathy and rest were necessary before the pain levels were manageable and he could begin to contemplate any more computer work.

The individual scenarios may be different from person to person – but the end result is always dis-stress.

How Can Aromatherapy Help Us to Combat Stress?

Let's face it: we will never be able to escape from stress. The milk pan is going to boil over whilst the children scream; the washing machine will break down in mid-wash; the train will be cancelled or signal workers' strike action will cause you to lose another day's pay; the business acquisition will not go according to plan; the job may be 'on the line'. All these things happen and will continue to happen.

For as long as we are alive we have to accept stress as part of living, just as we have to accept that germs are all around us. It is totally impossible to live in a sterile world – we live in a germ-laden environment. Yet, if our health is good, we can withstand viruses, bacteria and any of the billions of micro-organisms which have the potential to cause illness. In the same way we need to keep our health – mental, physical and spiritual – in good order so that we can rise above the daily onslaught of our stress-filled lives.

A beautiful analogy is that of the lotus flower, an

exquisite blossom that floats on the surface of muddy water but never gets tainted by it. Its roots are firmly attached to the bottom of the pond, and it is from there that the plant receives the nutrients necessary to sustain life. As the water level rises and falls the stem grows to allow the blossom always to float on the surface of the water – and no matter how dirty the water, the lotus flower always stays clean and beautiful.

The emotional and mental realm of human beings is complex and mysterious. Our minds can soar to the heights of ecstasy and sink to the depths of despair. Passion can race in our breasts, robbing the mind of rational thought. Our emotions defy precise definition and measurement, which is perhaps why science has split the mind from the body and focused on studying bodily functions, leaving the elusive mind and emotions out of the equation. But physicians down the ages have acknowledged the power of the mind to alter the outcome of disease, and it behoves us to understand the power and nature of our emotions.

Orthodox methods of dealing with stress fall roughly into two camps. There are those which society has adopted over several hundred years, which include drinking alcohol, smoking cigarettes and using recreational drugs; there are those prescribed by the medical establishment, which include sleeping tablets, tranquillisers and anti-depressants. Both approaches to combating stress attempt to fool the brain into thinking that everything is fine by temporarily blocking the messages of distress and disharmony. This is effected by chemical means on the principle that two things cannot occupy the same space at the same time. Although temporarily effective, these spurious ways of coping with stress are often taken to excess, causing addiction, poisoning and great harm to both mind and body, ultimately creating more stresses than they ever cured.

Aromatherapy doesn't claim to 'cure' us of stress, but it does achieve remarkable results in that it brings relief from stress without being addictive, anti-social or toxic.

Moreover, its legacy is one of wellbeing. Chapter 3 explains the different ways in which it works and describes what a powerful therapy it is.

As its name suggests, aromatherapy seeks to heal, make better and improve the quality of our life by the use of aromas. These are not just any aromas – coffee, after all, is very aromatic – but the fragrance of plants which have therapeutic properties. These plant aromas are called essential oils because they are the 'essence' of the plant. Although an essential oil can often be seen to act as powerfully as an allopathic drug, these oils are not drugs, and as such do not target one specific area of the body (an antacid, for instance, would only act to neutralise stomach acid). Essential oils work holistically, which means that they have a beneficial effect on the emotions and the body by restoring harmony and equilibrium, whilst simultaneously killing off bacteria and strengthening the immune system.

There are several ways to administer an essential oil but the most commonly used method is that of massaging the oils into the skin. It is for this reason that the word 'aromatherapy' invariably conjures up an image of 'fragrant massage'.

The Nurses' Stress Project

Many careers and occupations have heavy stress loads, but perhaps none more so than the nursing profession. Irrespective of the family or social stresses that a nurse may experience outside the hospital, within the confines of her job she faces the stresses of hard work, done on an anti-social, biorhythmically disturbing shift system, for low pay and in a germ-laden environment. Let's look at these factors in a little more detail.

A nursing contract stipulates that each nurse must work, in rotation, the early shift (8a.m. to 3p.m.), late shift (2p.m. to 10p.m.) and night shift (10p.m. to 8 a.m.). Effectively this means that nurses can never get into a pattern of day and night, light and dark, work and rest as the majority of us do. Their body rhythms become confused and as a result they suffer a sort of 'jet lag' as they constantly attempt to adjust.

Nursing is physically very demanding, and is the polar opposite of a desk job. Nurses are on their feet for long periods of time, and are also required to lift and turn patients who may be larger and heavier than they are themselves.

No one would enter nursing for the money. The poor pay means that nurses sometimes have to juggle their personal finances in order to pay the bills, or to take on some extra work (which often entails more nursing via the 'nurse bank' – a pool of off-duty nurses who can be called upon to fill in for absentee staff).

A large hospital naturally contains vast numbers of patients suffering from a wide range of disorders and diseases, and in a general hospital the nursing staff cannot avoid coming into contact with a multitude of micro-organisms. This puts a stress on the immune system and the ability of each individual nurse to stay healthy. Furthermore, the nursing contract only allows for a certain number of sick days per year, which means that once the quota has been reached either any illness must be worked through or, if time off is taken, money is lost.

Bearing in mind all these points, in 1994 I decided to undertake a nurses' stress project at my local hospital. I wanted to see, in a short period of time, just how effective aromatherapy could be in reducing stress levels, increasing wellbeing and building up resistence to illness. The project involved fifty volunteer nurses having a once-a-week massage lasting for approximately forty-five minutes. Twenty women from a local massage training school, who had been trained in basic massage, donated their time to assist in the trial.

Many of the nurses had never experienced a massage, although some were familiar with aromatherapy or had come into contact with the use of essential oils within a hospital ward. Before their massage treatment began all the nurses filled in questionnaires detailing their stress levels, sleep patterns and various other health matters. Each treatment consisted of a simple back and neck massage using one of three pre-blended massage oils. One blend was an 'energising' mixture; one contained essential oils known for their uplifting and soothing properties; and the third blend consisted of essential oils that fight infection and strengthen the immune system.

At the start of the trial the questionnaire revealed that 62 per cent of nurses felt that their stress levels were 'moderate', whilst 32 per cent stated that their stress levels were 'fairly high' to 'very high', accompanied by symptoms ranging from permanently sore throats to chronic insomnia. Common to almost every nurse, however, were backache, tense shoulders and a sore neck which got worse whenever they had to lift heavy objects. Tension in the neck and shoulders combined with lack of sleep caused many of the nurses to suffer from irritability, over-sensitivity and depression.

After only two or three massage sessions nurses were experiencing a reduction of pain in their necks, shoulders and backs. Sleep levels were vastly improved: one nurse reported that, instead of the two to four hours she was used to, she was now sleeping for six hours or more. Another nurse who had previously suffered from a sore throat for six days out of seven was surprised, during her third week of treatment, to find that her throat was now only sore for one or two days a week.

Questionnaires filled out after the trial, revealed mainly enthusiastic and positive feedback. Below is a selection of unsolicited comments.

I found the eight-week massage course totally therapeutic and looked forward to each one, knowing that I would feel better as a whole person.

I found it hard to believe how much stress affects our bodies, until I had my shoulders and neck massaged. They have never felt so good in ten years as a nurse.

I looked forward to the massage; to be completely relaxed for one hour was of great benefit.

I felt my stress levels were better and I could cope better.

I found the raised energy levels, better sleep and less infections ended when the massage ended. I'd gladly take part in another massage project.

I had been experiencing sleep disturbance for some time. However, the night of the sessions I certainly slept better and felt relaxed.

Since completing the trial, neck and shoulder ache has returned. During the trial this virtually disappeared and the actual neck movement was better than for years.

I suffer with eczema which improved dramatically, especially on my face.

I felt very laid back and little things didn't irritate me so much.

I found I learned to relax, and this was a great benefit in this busy world.

One nurse summed up the general feeling amongst the nursing staff taking part in the eight-week massage trial: I cannot thank you all enough for helping to improve my physical and psychological wellbeing.

Although I have been involved with aromatherapy for more than twenty years, and believe in it wholeheartedly, even I was surprised at the enthusiasm shown by the nurses. When only a quarter of the way through the trial, the majority of nurses taking part had experienced definite benefits and were discussing the feasibility of

regular aromatherapy massage sessions being incorporated into hospital life.

So you see how effective aromatherapy can be. It is also
highly practical, since it can be incorporated into the
daily routines of even the most over-worked and exhausted person: it isn't necessary to go off for a weekend
and be in a peaceful environment to enjoy the benefits of
aromatherapy. It can be taken into the workplace, into
the home, into the institution. The only things that are
needed are a treatment couch, a bottle of massage oil and
a loving touch. It does help to have taken a basic training
course in massage, but even without that any one of us
can help our partner, child, parent or friend to let go of
stress and to feel better in themselves. To experience
relaxation is to have a feeling of wellbeing. And when we
feel well and good about ourselves, we automatically find
it easier to cope with our stressful lives.

2

The Effects of Stress on Body, Mind and Emotions

Every day, millions of people visit their local general practitioner, seeking advice and medication for a health problem. GPs listen, look and advise. They frequently also prescribe drugs to treat the disease, malfunction or imbalance that has caused the patient to visit the surgery. Common health problems can range from indigestion to heart palpitations, from aches and pains to chronic fatigue, and may be variously labelled as irritable bowel syndrome, tachycardia, arthritis or TATT (Tired All The Time). But how many patients, when walking out of the surgery with a prescription in their hand, really understand the role of stress in their health problem?

It is becoming recognised that 90 per cent of our diseases and health problems are precipitated or exacerbated by stress – stresses caused to the body or mind from physical means (such as lifting heavy objects or sitting incorrectly), from mental anguish (such as a court battle for child custody) and from emotional pain (such as feelings of rejection, which may have its roots in childhood). But how does stress – whether of physical, mental or emotional origin – affect the body's ability to self-regulate and heal itself? And how can we, as individuals, look at what is taking place, understand what is taking place, and then become active participants in regenerating our own health?

Stress can cause a breakdown in any of the body systems – the immune system, nervous system, reproductive system, cardiovascular system, respiratory system, lymphatic system, digestive system or locomotor system. It does this by creating a chemical or structural imbalance in the body. Homeostasis (balance) is what the body constantly strives for (see fig. 1) and it is when this balance is disrupted that ill health follows.

This chapter attempts to explain, in relatively simple terms, the ways in which our body systems break down and begin to malfunction under stress, and how the pathological outcome of each breakdown is able to be labelled as 'this disease' or 'that disease'. When the body is looked at in this way, it starts to become clear why certain drugs are prescribed for particular conditions (such as cortisone for arthritis) – they are attempting to replace by artificial means the chemicals which should be, but are no longer, produced in sufficient quantities in the body. As you read this chapter you will begin to see how our body's chemical balance can become disturbed and how that imbalance can result in ill health. Once you have started to understand that process of destruction you may find the willpower and commitment to take control of your health and wellbeing, and to make whatever adjustments are necessary – to your diet, your lifestyle and your mental and emotional outlook – to enable the incredible machinery that is your body to repair itself so that you can regain and enjoy good health.

Our body is us, we are our body, and it may be rather difficult to think of our body systems objectively – after all, each one of us has been taking our body for granted for years. It may only be when ill health or disease strikes that we become aware that some part of our body is not working properly. For example, anyone suffering from cystitis or candida albicans may become acutely aware of the uro-genital system, and be conscious of how different foods and liquids affect the simple process of urination or the desire to engage in sexual intercourse.

Although the different body systems work in tandem

with each other they are outlined separately in medical textbooks, and medical students build up their knowledge of the workings of the human body by studying the individual systems. In this way it becomes possible to grasp the incredible complexity of the human body.

The Mind-Body Link

There is a strong relationship between the mind, life experiences, and the onset and outcome of disease. The study of these links is called psychoneuroimmunology or PNI.

When life events are experienced as stressful, they are processed in the cortex of the brain (which receives imput from all five of our senses – touch, sight, hearing, taste and smell) and information is relayed via the limbic system to the hypothalamus. This area of the brain rules the internal environment and regulates vegetative functions such as growth, reproduction, thyroid function, appetite and sleep. Neurosecretory cells in the hypothalamus release messenger molecules (neuropeptides) which travel to the pituitary gland and other parts of the brain. These messenger molecules modulate the release of many hormones including ACTH (adrenocorticotrophic hormone). ACTH amplifies distress signals by stimulating the release of powerful corticosteroids from the cortex of the adrenal gland.

Hypothalamic neurons simultaneously increase the activity of the sympathetic branch of the autonomic nervous system, causing a release of the catecholamines adrenaline and noradrenaline from the adrenal gland. Corticosteroids and catecholamines are known to impair the efficiency of the immune system because they reduce the activity of both macrophages and lymphocytes, leaving a person with a weakened defence system and increasing their susceptibility to disease (see fig. 2).

Figure 1   Homeostasis = Balance

The body is constantly trying to maintain a perfect balance of chemicals in our body – to supply more of those which we need and to reduce the amount of those which we don't need in such quantities. If nothing happens to interfere with that balance, the body can work efficiently to keep us healthy.

The ebbing and flowing of chemicals and hormones within the body could be likened to the water level in a tidal river: high tide, falling tide, low tide, rising tide – always changing, always on the move. If too much rain falls in a short period of time then at high tide the water can burst the banks of the river and cause widespread damage to surrounding areas. When flooding occurs the costs can be high in terms of physical destruction, financial losses, loss of livelihood and even loss of life. And when insufficient rains fall the river levels may fall so low that fish die and boats cannot set sail. In other words, when an unusual circumstance occurs the normal ebb and flow of the tides does not happen.

If we imagine a set of old-fashioned scales they would be constantly rising and falling to create a balance in the body's chemical and hormone levels. But if something interferes with that delicate balance, then too much or too little of vital chemicals/hormones are produced or released into the body systems, and this imbalance results in ill health, disease or death. This balance is called homeostasis, and the body is constantly seeking a balance.

SALT/WATER
In hot climates we consciously eat salt tablets to conserve water. Ordinarily too much salt causes water retention in the tissues.

HOT/COLD
When the weather is hot, we sweat to cool down. When the weather is cold we shiver to get warm. Our body keeps a constant temperature of 98.4 degrees.

SODIUM/POTASSIUM
Balance between these minerals dictates healthy cell growth.

BLOOD ALKALINITY/BLOOD ACIDITY

ALKALINITY OF URINE/ACIDITY OF URINE

RIF/HRF
Release Inhibiting Factor/Hormone Releasing Factor. Both send messages to hypophysis to release or inhibit hormones.

ADRENALINE/ACETYLCHOLINE
Produced in the adrenals. Andrenaline fires up the sympathetic nervous system. Acetylcholine is controlled by the para-sympathetic system.

INSULIN/GLUCOGEN
Both produced in the pancreas. Insulin lowers blood sugar levels, glucogen raises blood sugar levels.

CORTISONE/DES-OXY-CORTISONE (D.O.S)
Two chemicals produced in the adrenal glands. Cortisone is needed to depress inflammation, but too much will depress the immune system. Too little cortisone results in allergic reactions ie. inflammation. D.O.S is the antagonist of cortisone. It helps the body fight infection by setting up inflammation (eg around a boil) to prevent spread of infection. It prevents the over-production of cortisone.

SYMPATHETIC NERVOUS SYSTEM/
PARASYMPATHETIC NERVOUS SYSTEM
Antagonists to each other, these systems are explained fully in Chapter 2.

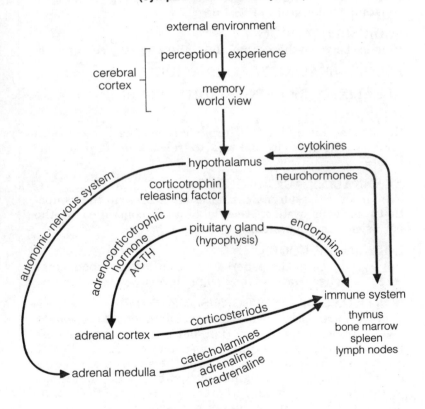

Figure 2

The Immune System

A healthy immune system is vital to the wellbeing and survival of all living creatures; in essence it is a surveillance system which is able to distinguish between 'self' and 'non-self' and to eliminate the latter, thus preserving the integrity of the former. Non-self includes all microorganisms, viruses, bacteria and parasites – foreign substances breathed in from the air and eaten in food. Cancer cells are non-self, and a fully competent immune system will recognise and destroy those cells before they can form tumours.

The cells of the immune system are widely distributed through all the tissues of the body, and are derived from the thymus, bone marrow, spleen and lymph nodes. They are classified according to their appearance and tissue of origin; the main classes of cells are B lymphocytes, T lymphocytes, natural killer cells (NK) and macrophages. Acting in unison they identify, inactivate and eliminate viruses, bacteria and other foreign material.

An important discovery is that the cells of the immune system are able to receive data from the hormones and messenger molecules produced by the brain in the stress response. Therefore the activity and competence of the immune system may be profoundly affected, via the nervous system, by emotional and mental states. In addition cytokines, messenger molecules produced by immune system cells, have a direct effect on the central nervous system.

Many studies have demonstrated that corticosteroids, whose levels are raised with stress, heavily suppress the cells of the immune system; but corticosteroids are not all bad – they also have a marked anti-inflammatory and anti-allergic action. When secreted in large amounts, corticosteroids inhibit many of the functions of lymphocytes, macrophages and leucocytes. A correct balance is what is desirable.

Stress raises the levels of adrenaline and noradrenaline, and these powerful molecules are known to depress immune system functions. It is also very likely that prolonged stress, associated with consistently raised levels of catecholamines, plays a major role in the generation of hypertension, heart attacks and strokes.

Endorphins or endogenous opiates are a large group of peptides which have been isolated from the brain and pituitary gland. Opiate levels are increased with stress; it has been shown that opiates decrease natural killer cell activity, and during prolonged stress they are immunosuppressive.

The Cardiovascular System

Diseases of the heart and blood vessels are now the major killer in industrialised societies, with ever-increasing incidence of heart attacks, angina, hypertension and strokes. The process often begins in early childhood with a diet high in animal fat and refined carbohydrates, and a lifestyle that includes very little physical exercise. In adult life the situation is exacerbated by smoking and a continued sedentary existence; all too often the result is premature death.

The underlying disease process starts with fatty deposits being laid down on the lining of arteries. The result is a narrowing of the arteries, leading to decreased blood flow to the tissue supplied by each artery, and a reduction in the supply of oxygen to the affected tissue.

In the case of very active tissue like the heart muscle, the demand for oxygen may exceed the capacity of the arteries to deliver. So the heart suffers, giving rise to the characteristic pain of angina. During exercise and at times of strong emotion the heart rate, and therefore the oxygen demand, may easily outstrip the capacity of the arteries to deliver sufficient oxygen, and in severe cases parts of the muscle will die. The rough surface of the fatty deposits on the artery walls encourages the formation of clots, and if a major artery is blocked a large area of tissue dies. The result may be a heart attack, a stroke or a limb going gangrenous.

Stress plays a major role in the development of blood vessel disease. Stress makes people feel bad, and in a misguided attempt to feel better they may smoke or overeat. Stress also interferes with homeostasis (the body's ability to maintain a healthy balance of body fluids, chemicals and hormones); blood acidity/alkalinity levels (which determine the thickness of the blood); the sodium/potassium balance of the body cells (which affects not only the blood pressure but also fluid retention in the tissues); and the metabolism of cholesterol. Serious problems arising from these imbalances include coronary thrombosis, high blood pressure (which can lead to a stroke) or heart attack.

The Autonomic Nervous System

The main function of the autonomic nervous system (ANS) is to regulate the functioning of the internal organs, and keep the body in a state of homeostasis (balance). The ANS consists of the sympathetic nervous system and the parasympathetic nervous system. Noradrenaline is the nerve messenger of the sympathetic nervous system; acetylcholine is the nerve messenger of the parasympathetic system.

Stimulation of the sympathetic nervous system results from bodily activity – fright, danger, a threat of some description – and can be brought into play by any stressful encounter. Whether that encounter is made via the sense of touch, taste, smell, sound or sight, the response format is always the same: the blood pressure rises, the heart rate and respiration increase to enable us to run faster, our pupils dilate so that we have sharper vision, sugar stored in the liver is released into the bloodstream to provide energy for our muscles, our hair bristles, and we perspire more in order to cool down the skin.

Simultaneously any bodily functions that are not necessary to the flight from danger or fight for life or rights (the fight-or-flight response) are greatly decreased. The body has deployed energy from certain body systems to make other systems more effective. Suddenly digestion of food is not essential; consequently movement of food through the stomach and intestines is decreased, as is the secretion of digestive juices by the intestinal glands.

These stress responses have been the same since prehistoric man needed to run from a forest fire, fight off a rival for his cavewoman or kill a dangerous animal for food. Useful though it often still is, there are many situations in modern living when the stress response is not helpful since it cannot be utilised in any practical way – such as when we are trying to collect a child from school and getting stuck in a traffic jam; when our boss is over-critical or over-demanding, and we dare not respond for fear of losing our job and our financial security; or when we are sitting in front of the television, trying to unwind after a tiring day, and the news bulletin reports a new disaster but are helpless to intervene. The body does not discriminate, but re-creates the stress response of our ancestors by stimulating the sympathetic nervous system – even though we have nothing to fight and nothing to run away from.

On winning the fight or slaying the animal our ancestors would experience an instant sense of relief – possibly even euphoria at having emerged triumphant. This feeling would trigger the parasympathetic nervous system to take over from the sympathetic nervous system, and harmony would be restored within the body (see fig. 3). The parasympathetic nervous system slows the heartbeat, restores respiration to normal, contracts the pupils, relaxes muscles which have been tensed during 'fight mode' and releases the mind from its concentration. It

AUTONOMIC NERVOUS SYSTEM

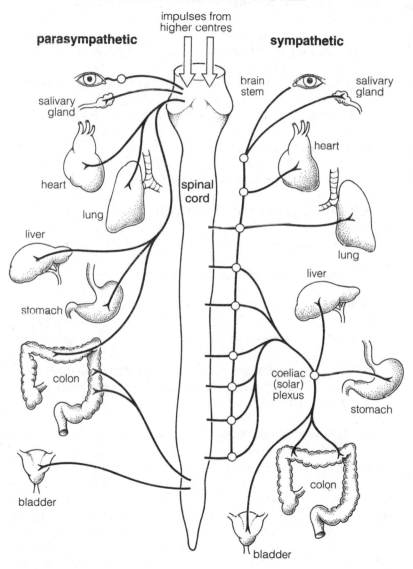

Figure 3

Figure 3A
**Action of Parasympathetic Nervous System
to restore harmony after stressful event is over**

- Breathing slows down.

- Senses (eyes, ears and brain) lose their acuteness.

- Stomach and intestines work to digest food.

- Defecation is possible.

- Heartbeat returns to normal.

- Salivation returns to normal.

- Hormonal function returns to normal.

- Adrenaline production ceases.

- Body feels tired.

- Brain may 'switch off'.

- Blood leaves arms and legs to return to abdominal organs (and to break down the stress hormones – adrenaline etc.).

- Muscles relax (legs may go wobbly).

Action of the Sympathetic Nervous System in response to stress

- Heartbeat increases.

- Tubes to lungs expand.

- Spleen releases extra blood cells.

- Digestion stops.

- Blood moves from abdominal organs to the organs responsible for muscular exertion.

- Muscular fatigue is abolished as sugar (stored in the liver) is released into the bloodstream.

- Adronal glands are stimulated to pour adrenaline into the bloodstream.

- Adrenaline gives heightened awareness to brain, eyes and ears.

- Salivation ceases.

- Skin feels clammy as sweat is poured out.

- Muscles twitch ready for exertion.

- Hormones (such as growth hormone and sex hormones) are not released into the bloodstream.

governs the metabolism of the body and the rebuilding of bodily energy reserves (ready for the next demanding situation). The digestion and elimination processes start to work efficiently again, which allows the body to excrete toxic wastes created by the stress response. Ancient man would at this point most probably have taken a large drink of water to quench his thirst, which would further enhance the natural detoxifying action of the body.

Sadly for us today, we rarely experience euphoria at the end of a stressful experience, as modern stresses tend to permeate our everyday lives to create worry, anxiety and an inability to relax and feel peaceful. As a result we are governed by our sympathetic nervous system for most of the time.

The Reproductive System

In medical books the reproductive system is commonly lumped together with the urinary system and the combination is called the uro-genital system. The kidneys govern the production and discharge of urine and, as such, are also a part of the uro-genital system. Urine should not be alkaline, but slightly acidic, as the acid nature of urine kills bacteria and flushes it from the body before it can create a health hazard. This is very important in an area of our anatomy where new human life can be created. Stress can make the blood too alkaline, which in turn creates urine which is too alkaline and is therefore unable to protect the genitalia against infection from micro-organisms.

The reproductive system, like all other body systems, is under the control of the hypothalamus, the command centre of the brain. After sensory messages have passed through the cerebral cortex, via the limbic system, it is the job of the hypothalamus to interpret them and send either 'red alert' messages via the sympathetic nervous system or messages to the gonads to the effect that it is safe to reproduce (see fig 4.)

The hypothalamus produces what is known as Release Inhibiting Factor (RIF) if there is stress and the sympathetic nervous system is dominant, and Hormone Releasing Factor (HRF) if the parasympathetic system is dominant. Nature has designed us so that we put our own survival before procreation – it would not be sensible to do otherwise – which means that if we are under stress and experiencing anxiety, fear or exhaustion our sex response will be depressed. Sex hormones (gonadotropic hormones) are produced in the hypophysis and released into the bloodstream only when instructed by HRF from the hypothalamus. Once diffused into the bloodstream these hormones, amongst other things, stimulate ovulation and the production of testosterone. A women under severe stress will cease to ovulate and probably also cease to menstruate. Lack of testosterone will affect men and women alike – the sex drive will be sadly lacking. Spermatozoa are stimulated by Leydig's interstitial cells, which are in turn stimulated by the hypophysis, which as already explained is ultimately controlled by the hypothalamus. Too much stress in modern life may account for the decline in fertility – a crucial topic if the human race is to survive.

The Locomotor System

Stress, whether emotional, mental or physical in origin, causes muscle tension which can create further physical problems. These problems may manifest as lower back pain, stiff neck and consequent headaches, frozen shoulder, or sciatica (when uneven muscular tension forces the skeleton to tilt or twist slightly, thus pressing on nerves).

Figure 4

Effects of long-term stress on reproductive system

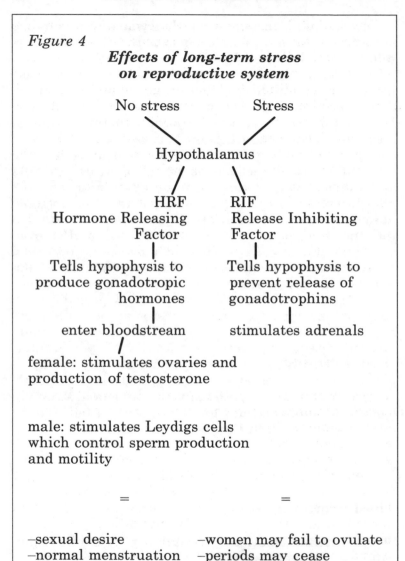

No stress   Stress

Hypothalamus

HRF   RIF
Hormone Releasing   Release Inhibiting
Factor   Factor

Tells hypophysis to   Tells hypophysis to
produce gonadotropic   prevent release of
hormones   gonadotrophins

enter bloodstream   stimulates adrenals

female: stimulates ovaries and
production of testosterone

male: stimulates Leydigs cells
which control sperm production
and motility

=   =

–sexual desire   –women may fail to ovulate
–normal menstruation –periods may cease
–fertility   –fertility is lessened
                    –libido is dampened
                    –sexual response
                      diminished

Physical problems such as lower back pain account for millions of lost work days per year, and cost industry and the country billions of pounds in sickness benefits and lost productivity. As well as lost income and constant pain, this condition prevents large numbers of people from performing normal everyday tasks and enjoying sports, exercise and sexual activity. Inability to work or enjoy life to the full can produce further stress, and the person concerned may become depressed, irritable and unable to sleep. Medical help may be sought and, quite apart from the cost to the National Health Service of providing painkillers, anti-depressants, sleeping tablets and so on, a further problem now arises. The sufferer not only has to cope with a stress-induced physical disability, but his or her immune system will, under the influence of prescription drugs, become less efficient.

The Lymphatic System

This system is so essential to our health that if it were to cease functioning for twenty-four hours we would die. All waste material from the body's continual renewing of cells, metabolising of nutrients and release of toxic wastes is carried away in the lymph, to the organs responsible for elimination – kidney, liver and the gut. The lymph is a colourless fluid which comes from the bloodstream and subsequently returns there. As lymph flows through the body's lymph nodes it picks up lymphocytes which are manufactured in the nodes. These lymphocytes travel through the lymphatic system, always ready to attack and kill any invading pathogen such as bacteria or viral material. Lymph rejoins the blood when it reaches the chest (just beneath the collar bone).

If we think of the body as a large hotel, the lymphatic system could be likened to the chambermaids. Every day they clean all the rooms and take away rubbish. They destroy odours and dirt and try to remove any trace of the previous guests. They then bring fresh supplies of laundry, soap, tissues and so on so that each room can be used by a new guest. Without this daily cleansing a hotel would just be a building full of disgusting rubbish and no one would want to stay there. It would soon go out of business.

A sluggish lymphatic system spells trouble for the body. Fluids and toxins accumulate in the tissues. Excess fats will cease to be taken away and will cause the body to put on weight. Many factors contribute to a less than competent lymphatic system – one of those factors being stress. Lethargy and depression are often the legacy of a stressful period in our lives, and under these conditions the lymphatic system works less efficiently. When daily toxins are unable to be taken away by the lymph they are dumped in body tissues, or they cause problems by clogging up the lymph nodes, which in turn hampers the production of lymphocytes. Our immune system becomes impaired and therefore our resistance to disease is lessened. Our body shape and size may get out of hand, which can cause further stress as we become depressed by the sight of ourselves in the mirror.

The Digestive System

Also known as the alimentary system, the digestive system deals with our nutrition from the moment we see or smell food (it makes us salivate) to eating food (chewing and swallowing) and then to the digestion of food in the stomach (by dissolving it in hydrochloric acid). From the stomach the food then passes into the small intestine where further juices help the process of digestion, and it is from here that nutrients are absorbed into the bloodstream and circulate throughout the body to repair and renew every cell. Whatever is not wanted by the body is then pushed into the large intestine by peristaltic action, and is eventually excreted along with toxic waste products such as dead blood cells, which is a natural daily occurrence.

This process is temporarily stopped when the sympathetic nervous system primes the body for defensive action (see p. 29) and normally, when the danger is over, the process of digestion continues. Problems arise, however, when our stress loads create a permanent state of anxiety – when the sympathetic nervous system is constantly producing those chemicals which suppress or depress the digestive process.

Under long-term conditions of stress, many states of ill health arise. Fear suppresses the production of saliva – we get a dry mouth. In prehistoric man this meant that he had no need to swallow whilst running away from danger; translated into today's lifestyle, it means that we either constantly seek to compensate by drinking cup after cup of coffee, or we lose our appetite and start to become malnourished.

Stomach Acid

In order to digest food we have to produce enough stomach acid, yet we often seek to suppress this process by swallowing antacid tablets. Eating hurriedly, 'on the trot' and too late in the evening can all lead to a feeling of 'acid indigestion', simply because our body tension is preventing the part-digested food from passing into the small intestine and consequently we feel uncomfortable. Many people suffer because they produce too little stomach acid (which also gives a feeling of discomfort); and this may mistakenly lead them to take antacid tablets, which will further depress the body's ability to digest food.

Under normal circumstances hydrochloric acid is constantly secreted by the stomach. It helps to regulate the opening and closing of the stomach, and also enters the small intestine where it stimulates the production of secretin by the glands in the first part of the small intestine. Secretin acts to increase the flow of pancreatic juices and bile, which digest fat. Reduced stomach acid will therefore also reduce these secretions. Without proper digestion the body cannot absorb all the nutrients from the food, which passes into the large intestine where it creates excess gas and is eventually excreted. Low stomach acid is very common in middle age – coincidental with 'middle age spread', which occurs when the body is not metabolising food as efficiently as before.

The kidneys are central organs of metabolism. They decide what the body will excrete and what will be retained for regeneration.

Constipation

This extremely common problem is caused primarily by eating too many processed foods. Stress plays its part by keeping the body in a near-permanent state of 'alertness' and interfering with the peristaltic action which should move food on. In the hope of finding an instant solution we turn to laxatives instead of seeking to address the real problems – the need to eat good food and to give our body the chance to perform its job of digestion by sitting down and taking time to eat. Anyone who has 'suffered' from constipation will understand the meaning of the word. It is a form of poisoning, as the body needs to get rid of wastes in order to remain healthy. Toxic wastes which cannot be excreted become reabsorbed by the body, and this can contribute to cellulite, bad breath and offensive-smelling perspiration. If constipation is severely chronic it could ultimately lead to septicaemia (blood poisoning).

Sick Headaches

The vagus nerve is the principal nerve of the parasympathetic nervous system, and forms a direct link from the brain to the stomach for transmitting messages of digestion. At times of extreme or prolonged stress this information channel stops working and we can become nauseous, dizzy, over-sensitive to noise or motion, and saddled with dull, persistant, excruciating headache – a classic 'sick headache'. This condition can even cause vomiting.

A Chain Is Only as Strong as Its Weakest Link

The human body works by an incredible process of inter-linked systems, all nourished by the bloodstream and all served by the nervous system. In a healthy human being each of the body systems operates at optimum efficiency. Under stress conditions, as already described, the body systems fail to operate properly and things start to go wrong. What ultimately goes wrong, and in which system, may depend on a variety of factors including genetics, environment, diet, general lifestyle and medication, prescribed or otherwise.

For example, ten people working for the same boss in the same company, and all experiencing high stress levels, may all become ill, but in different ways. The person who develops Crohn's disease has a weakness in the digestive system which may have its roots in childhood. The person who suffers a minor heart attack has a weakness in the cardiovascular system which may be related to diet, drinking habits or lack of exercise. A woman may suffer from dysmenorrhoea or find that she has fibroids and needs to undergo a hysterectomy; if she has pursued her career, hoping to have a child later, the news will be devastating. Someone else may develop cancer, and there seems to be a cancer for every organ, orifice and area of the body. Other workers may suffer a nervous breakdown if they push themselves way beyond their capabilities, and, after using up their energy reserves, fail to see that they need to rebuild these reserves and start instead to live on nervous energy. Nervous energy is only meant to be used in times of emergency; when it becomes a part of everyday living that person comes to an abrupt halt, just as when a car runs out of petrol.

The stressful situation may be the same for each person. The stress response through the body's sympathetic nervous system, may also be identical. After that, the routing of destructive energy will target the weakest area in the body and, by causing a pathological breakdown, will reveal itself in the form of a particular ailment.

A chain is only as strong as its weakest link; when an outside force is exerted on it the chain must be uniformly strong to do its job. So it is with us. Stress will always be with us, and will exert its force upon us. But if we take control of every aspect of our lives – sleeping, eating and drinking, exercising, talking about our fears and anxieties, and tackling small problems with alternative therapies rather than waiting until the complaint needs medical intervention – we can stay disease-free, healthy and whole.

3

How Essential Oils Reduce Stress

What Is an Essential Oil?

Before you can understand how essential oils work on the body, you need to understand the nature of an essential oil. Although known as an oil, it is not like engine oil, baby oil, frying oil or salad oil. An essential oil is non-greasy, does not prevent friction and is non-lubricating. It is a unique substance, part liquid and part gas: in other words, it is a volatile oil. It is fragrant and its molecules are lighter than air – therefore it evaporates, dissipating fragrance into its immediate atmosphere. Although all essential oils evaporate into the air, they do so at different rates. Some essential oils, such as lemon, are very thin and watery and evaporate quickly; others, such as sandalwood, are quite thick - more like the consistency of honey – and evaporate very slowly. So the viscosity (thickness) of an essential oil determines how quickly it will evaporate.

Where Do Essential Oils Come From?

Essential oils are contained within plants, or parts of plants. We are all familiar with the zest of lemon, orange or grapefruit which is contained within the skin and remains hidden until the peel is cut. Lovers of various oriental cuisines will be aware of the fragrance of spices such as black pepper, cardamom and coriander, all of which contain essential oils. Essential oil-containing spices and fruits can all be found in the local high street, and even in our gardens there is a whole range of essential oil-containing plants. Lavender is a familiar plant, as is peppermint (a variety of which enhances the taste of new potatoes) and, of course, the fragrant rose.

Essential oils are usually removed from the plant by distillation. This process involves passing high-pressure steam through the plant material so that the fragrance, being liquid, is removed; after this mixture of steam and essential oil has cooled, the essential oil can easily be separated from it as oil floats on water.

The Qualities of an Essential Oil

An essential oil is a liquid as well as a gas, and as such it is able to work in unique ways. Because it is a gas and dissipates into the air, it is drawn into the body when we breathe; so any essential oil in the immediate environment will be drawn in through the nose. Some will reach the lungs after passing through the bronchial tubes, and, having joined forces with oxygen there, it will diffuse into the bloodstream.

Not all of the fragrance, however, will descend to the chest area. Tiny molecules travel through the nasal membranes (the olfactory epithelium) and penetrate the underlying tissue which is home to millions of olfactory receptors. These receptors tell us whether the smell is good or bad, and can differentiate between thousands of odours. Nerve fibres then transmit information to the limbic system in the brain, which forms an interface between the cerebral cortex and the 'master' glands of the endocrine system – the hypophysis (pituitary) and the hypothalamus. These glands, as discussed in Chapter 2, are responsible for the production and distribution of hormones such as the reproductive hormone gonadotropin. The hypothalamus, although only comprising 0.3 per cent of the brain, is involved in the body's regulation of temperature (shivering and perspiration); in appetite and thirst; in growth; in blood sugar levels; in sleeping and waking; in emotions (pleasure and anger, for example); and in the cycles of the reproductive system. It is also the control centre of the autonomic nervous system.

How Essential Oils work in the Body

Being liquid, essential oils are able to mix with other liquids. They are particularly suited to blending with fatty oils such as sweet almond oil, and, because of their ability to dissipate in fats, oils, liquid waxes and lotions, it is very easy to make a massage blend and to apply essential oils to the skin. Essential oils are very concentrated and therefore must only be used after first being diluted in a suitable base. For massage, the recommended proportion of essential oil to be added to fatty oil is 1–2 per cent.

The human body, although composed largely of water, also contains large amounts of lipids (fats), and for this reason essential oils travel easily throughout the body. Essential oils are said to be lipophilic – they love fats – and, having been applied to the skin, quickly penetrate the outer layer or epidermis and travel into the lower layer, the dermis.

All essential oils are antiseptic to one degree or another, and when massaged into the skin they immediately confer some protection against external infection. Like the glovers of sixteenth-century France who survived the plague because their occupation involved daily contact with essential oils – used to cure and perfume leather

before crafting gloves for members of fashionable society
– those who give or receive aromatherapy treatment on a
regular basis automatically become more resilient to
infections.

The lymphatic system is another medium in which
essential oils are carried through the body. Like a constantly ebbing and flowing tide which circulates through
the body tissues, lymph has two distinct functions – it
brings fresh lymphocytes to fight infections, and it takes
away the debris of cell renewal, toxins and unwanted fats.
When essential oils diffuse into the body they mix with
lymph and are transported on the same journey. As lymph
is a major component of the body's immune system it is
easy to see how essential oils are able to strengthen
resistance to disease, enhance the action of the immune
system and keep us healthy. Lymph travels throughout
the entire body, which means that essential oils also have
access to every nook and cranny of the person who
regularly uses them, whether in massage, bathing compresses or by inhalation.

Massage

The harm caused by stress can be undone by massage. A
prolonged period of stress, as explained earlier, will
cause the sympathetic nervous system to maintain a
constant vigil. The parasympathetic nervous system is
antagonistic to the sympathetic nervous system, which
means that when one system is in operation the other is
not. Since massage brings the parasympathetic nervous
system into play, it instantly reduces the power of the
sympathetic nervous system.

Massage tells the body it is not in danger. Like a crying
baby that stops crying when it is picked up because it
feels safe and comforted, when we are being massaged the
soothing, rhythmic movements send messages to our

autonomic nervous system that we are not in danger. Messages from the brain signal to the body that no adrenaline needs to be produced as there is no need to run away. Tense muscles are coaxed into relaxing – there is no reason for the muscles to stay tense, and so on. Messages are sent back to the hypothalamus – the body is in a receptive state, and hormones can be released. In effect, the sympathetic nervous system has had the volume turned down sufficiently for the parasympathetic nervous system to be heard.

We could liken the body to a sophisticated stereo music centre that has been designed to play every kind of music and is self-adjusting so that the music always sounds beautiful and pleasant to the ear. But stress interferes with the balance of sound and harmony disappears, giving way to an over-accentuated bass beat. The beautiful melody can no longer be heard and our appreciation of the music is lost because all that can be heard is the thump of the bass note. Eventually we start to think that this is music, and that it has to be accepted.

Aromatherapy massage could be likened to the graphic equaliser on a stereo, which allows you to turn down the bass and turn up the treble – to re-create a harmony of sound. Aromatherapy massage combines the sense of touch with the powerful therapeutic effect of essential oils. Dependent upon the essential oil chosen, remarkable results can be achieved – camomile or lavender, for example, will calm inflammation. Marjoram, melissa and vetivert are sedative oils and will quickly relax tense muscles. Oils of rosemary, black pepper and myrtle are excellent for rubbing into aching, tired limbs and will also bring pain relief to arthritic joints. Just remember, that essential oils are very concentrated and therefore quite powerful and must always be used sparingly. The recommended dosage is 1–3 drops of essential oil to every teaspoon of sweet almond oil.

4

Eat Well and Be Well

When we are under stress and finding it difficult to cope
with a host of demands it is very easy to skip meals,
grabbing a cup of coffee and a doughnut instead, or to
survive on ready-meals and takeaways. These foods may
be tasty and satisfy our hunger, but they are not always
nutritious. Our body needs nutrients from which to
rebuild cells, purify our blood and protect us from disease.

Aromatherapy, as seen in Chapter 3, has the potential
to restore harmony, fight infection, calm inflammation
and lift the spirits so that healing can take place – but,
powerful though essential oils and massage are, there are
some things that aromatherapy cannot rectify. A person
who has crawled through the desert will undoubtedly
benefit from aromatherapy if he has sore knees, as many
essential oils are bactericidal. However, his immediate
needs are for water and, shortly afterwards, for food. His
body is starving: craving food and water, without which
he will very soon die. The basis of our blood, lymph,
saliva, tears, and urine is water. Our body is just a
collection of cells which are dependent for their survival
upon vitamins, minerals, proteins, carbohydrates, fats
and sugars obtained from the food we eat. If we do not
eat well, then all the therapies in the world will not make
us healthy. Eating well means eating real foods and
drinking sufficient pure water to satisfy the body's needs.

Good Food Goes Off!

The longer a food is made to last, generally speaking, the less good it is for you. To make food keep it has to be pasteurised, freeze dried, heat-treated, homogenised or processed in some way. To put it simply, it is better to eat the oranges than the marmalade.

When shopping in the local supermarket it is difficult to glance into passing trolleys without feeling a little depressed. Many people seem to have lost the instinct to feed themselves properly and have become ensnared by seductive advertising, impulse buying and the ease of convenience food. The healthiest meals are those that are made from raw, fresh ingredients, organically grown if possible, because then your body is receiving whole living foods, rather than broken down, altered and preserved once-upon-a-time foods. If you go out to work, then make quick meals on weekdays and more time-consuming ones at the weekend. And remember, food manufacturers do not make processed food to improve your health but to make profits for themselves.

What Should a Healthy Larder Contain?

Basic foods for larder and fridge:

- Butter, organic if possible. Pesticides are concentrated in animal fats, so organic is best.
- Olive oil, extra virgin organic if you can afford it.
- Sesame oil, cold pressed.
- Free-range eggs.
- Free-range, organic meat (if you eat meat).
- Fresh fish.
- Organic yogurt.

- Small amounts of cheese, (cow, sheep or goat), organic if possible (see Butter, above).
- Tofu (a highly nutritious protein made from soya beans).
- Pulses, beans etc.
- Alfalfa seeds (for sprouting).
- Whole grains: rice, buckwheat, millet, barley.
- Wholewheat flour or, if you are allergic to wheat, spelt flour or gluten-free flour. Spelt flour is that which has not been genetically changed. Whenever possible, buy flour which is organic. Most of the grains sold for daily consumption in bread, cakes, biscuits and bags of flour have been stored and protected with ethylene di-chloride – a carcinogen).
- Flaked grains, e.g. oats and barley for muesli.
- Nuts: almonds, pecans, walnuts, hazelnuts (but they must be eaten fresh, before they acquire any bitter or rancid taste).
- Seeds: pumpkin seeds, sunflower seeds, sesame seeds, linseed etc. (as with nuts, seeds should be eaten before they go rancid).
- Sweeteners: molasses, honey, muscovado sugar, fructose, malt extract, maple syrup.
- Dried fruits: raisins, sultanas, apricots, figs, etc. (avoid those fruits which are treated with sulphur dioxide or mineral oils).
- Seaweed: arame, dulse, kombu, nori. These are useful and tasty in soups and stir-fries.
- Herbs and spices, black pepper, herb salt, low salt, sea salt.
- Rice cakes.
- Wholemeal bread (organic if possible). Alternatively, make your own.

There is no need to buy everything at once. Just stop buying convenience foods or refined foods and, when you run out, replace with healthy alternatives.

Essential Nutrients

As you will have noticed, there are relatively few convenience foods on the above list. It may look as though
you will have to spend a lot more time and effort in the
kitchen to prepare a meal, but there are plenty of ways
around this apparent drawback. Most vegetables, for
instance, can be cooked in minutes, or eaten raw. Car-
rots sliced into thin fingers or diagonally will cook faster
than when cut in rings, and retain more nutrients. Rice
and other whole grains will cook overnight in a large-
necked vacuum flask. Just warm the flask, tip in a cup of
rice or other grain and top up with boiling water. Grains
cooked in this way can be used cold for a lunchtime salad
or reheated later in the day. Obviously, cooking meals
from raw ingredients requires more skill than ripping
open a ready cooked meal, but if you are not familiar with
the techniques there are many excellent wholefood coo-
kery books available which will show you how to make
your own soups, sauces, pastry and so on.

The essential amino acids or EAAs are needed for tissue
repair and healthy functioning of the nervous system,
immune system, endocrine system, circulatory system
and the liver, which has the greatest need of EAAs.
Whether you eat meat or are vegetarian, it is vital to
obtain sufficient of the eight EAAs every day, since our
bodies cannot manufacture these nutrients themselves. All
eight are found in protein from meat, fish, eggs and dairy
foods, but if you are vegetarian or vegan you can obtain
them from whole grains and pulses or grains and nuts.
However, grains, pulses and nuts do not, individually,
contain all eight EAAs, so you must eat them together.
Then, they are as complete as beef or any other whole
protein. As an example of the simplicity of combining
incomplete proteins to provide the body with the full range
of essential amino acids, you can eat beans on toast, lentil
curry with almond pilaf, or even a peanut butter sandwich.

Equally important are the vitamins, minerals, trace

elements and fatty acids. These too are usually found in nuts, seeds, grains and vegetables, as well as in meat, fish and so on. And once again it is not necessary to eat dairy foods in order to obtain calcium. Almonds and other nuts and seeds contain quite adequate supplies of calcium, magnesium, phosphorus, zinc, vitamin B6, vitamin E and fatty acids. Calcium is also to be found in green leafy vegetables, especially in the stalks and ribs of leaves: just as calcium is located mostly in our skeleton, so it is also in the 'skeleton' of green leafy vegetables. Middle-age does not need to bring worries about osteoporosis, as long as the diet contains adequate amounts of calcium-rich foods. One of the richest sources of calcium is sesame seeds, which can be eaten in the form of tahini. This middle Eastern staple paste, made by crushing the sesame seeds to release the oils and minerals, is a vital ingredient in hummous.

Most pulses and seeds, such as alfalfa, will sprout easily and quickly, and are at their peak of goodness when eaten in this form: the vitamins, minerals and amino acids increase by 300 per cent, and the enzymes which make them digestible are also increased. Since beans and seeds vary in the length of time they need to be soaked before sprouting, it is advisable to obtain an instruction leaflet from a health food shop.

The Fats Debate

Which is better, butter or margarine? And do we eat too much fat altogether? These simple questions produce surprisingly complex and contradictory answers.

According to the government-commissioned NACNE report, today's diet in Europe and North America consists of 42 per cent fat, although the World Health Organisation recommends only 32 per cent fat. In the seventeenth century the average European diet contained about 20 per cent fat, whereas today it is only the Japanese who can boast a low fat diet – estimated at between 15 and 20 per cent.

Looking at these statistics it is easy to see that we do consume too much fat altogether – but which type of fat is better or worse for us? On the down-side, butter is quite low in essential fatty acids and contains about one gram of cholesterol per pound. It may also contain antibiotics (fed to cattle to protect them from illness), pesticides (on pasture land and in other cattle foods) and hormones (fed to cattle to increase growth and speed maturity). On the up-side, butter is not easily damaged by light and heat, so reducing the risk of introducing free radicals into the diet (see p. 52). Butter does contain some trans fatty acid (the part of butter that remains solid at room temperature; see also below), but in a form that can be metabolised by the body. Butter which comes from cattle raised organically, will, on balance, be better for you than a vegetable margarine.

Vegetable spreads begin life containing a good percentage of essential fatty acids (EFA). These fats are, as their name suggests, essential to life; amongst other functions they are used by the body to protect nerve endings, to make healthy cells and to maintain a normal hormone balance. Unfortunately, the process of partial hydrogenation (see medical dictionary) turns these essential fatty acids into trans fatty acids. Trans fatty acids are only useful to the body as fuel for energy. If we are active we can burn them off, although it is harder for our bodies to use these altered fats than to use the fats in butter. Our bodies cannot, however, use these fatty acids to renew hormones, cells or nerves.

Trans fats are implicated in the cause or worsening of cardiovascular and many inflammatory and degenerative diseases. The average Western diet contains approximately 10 lb of trans fats per year, which is more than the total yearly consumption of additives, colourings and flavourings.

Margarine is promoted as a health food high in polyunsaturates and low in saturated fats and cholesterol, and although manufacturers do use polyunsaturated oils they are not quality cold pressed oils of the kind which are readily usable by the body. The oils used for margarine have been extracted from the seeds or bean through chemical means or heat, and have lost their vitamin content in the process. Without these naturally occurring vitamins, our bodies cannot metabolise the oils in these spreads. Often, however, vitamins are added.

Butter has been part of the human diet since cattle were first domesticated, so it is unlikely that butter or cholesterol alone are the cause of all the degenerative diseases that have become epidemic over the past one hundred years. Margarine, after all, was only invented in the 1890s. On balance, organic butter is far more healthy than margarine – unless, of course, you happen to be allergic to dairy produce, a problem that is currently affecting 5 per cent of the population. In this case you will need to find a margarine that contains cold pressed oils (try health food stores), use it sparingly and do not use it for frying. Instead, choose olive or sesame oil (see p. 46).

Many foods containing vegetable fats or hydrogenated oils are unhealthy. The list is endless and includes many processed meals, whether from a supermarket or health food shop, biscuits, cakes, chocolates and sweets, vegan and vegetarian dairy-free foods (unless stated to the contrary), synthetic cream, coffee creamers and so on. Read labels to see how much these altered fats are used – you will be surprised just how frequently they crop up in our day-to-day diet. If you really want all the facts at your fingertips before making a decision about whether to switch from hydrogenated oils, read a book called *Fats and Oils* (see Further Reading). You may never want to eat deep-fried foods or margarine again.

Free Radicals, the Chemical Rapists

Every day of our lives, in biochemical reactions our bodies make and use potentially damaging substances called free radicals. Healthy people are able to protect themselves as long as their diet contains enough vitamin E, carotene, vitamin C and selenium. A healthy, nutritious diet will provide us with enough to deal with these self-generated free radicals, but the trouble begins when we start taking in free radicals in our food. When this happens we do not have enough healthy nutrients in our diet to protect us from the damaging effects.

What are free radicals, and how are they formed in our food? A free radical is a molecule with a missing electron which has been split off by some interference – chemically induced, high temperature frying, oxygenation of food, burning (as in toasting and barbecuing). Electrons have to be paired, and therefore the single electron will grab at the nearest molecule to steal one. This will lead to a chain reaction of electron-stealing.

Polyunsaturated oils are very vulnerable to free radical damage and this happens when the oil is in contact with heat, light or oxygen. So a bottle of oil sitting on a supermarket shelf can be made unhealthy just by light shining through the glass bottle. Light is the greatest enemy of fatty oils: it speeds up the reaction of oxygen and oil a thousand times, resulting in rancidity. Oxygen alone can cause fatty oils to go rancid. And when fatty oils are heated to high temperatures, it causes trans fats to form. All this is bad news for our bodies. When these fatty oils are used in our food the free radicals rob electrons from our very body cells, causing a destructive chain reaction throughout the body. This is believed to be one of the causes of arthritis, heart disease, arteriosclerosis and some cancers.

We all need the essential fatty acids found in polyunsaturates, but we need to eat the oil in its natural state – as nuts and seeds. Sunflower and pumpkin seeds can be added to cereals and salads, and we can eat small but regular amounts of almonds, walnuts, pecans and so on. These whole foods contain vitamin E which protects the EFAs from oxidation. Nature has added an antioxidant into the food so that the EFAs in nuts and seeds can be available to us for some time after they have been harvested.

If possible, buy oils in tins and only cook with olive and sesame oils as these are more hardy and less prone to chemical changes taking place when heated. It is also advisable to take an antioxidant supplement to help protect our body cells from free radical damage.

What if We Eat Well but Still Don't Feel Well?

Malfunction of the digestive tract is common, and you can eat the healthiest available diet and yet not benefit from it. If you feel bloated after eating or you have indigestion after most meals you are probably not getting the nutrition you should be getting from your food, because you are not assimilating the nutrients and they are largely passing through you.

Low stomach acid, known as hypochlorhydria by the medical profession, is frequently encountered. It is caused by a variety of reasons – stress, poor diet, smoking cannabis, drinking too much alcohol or eating too much protein. The symptoms resemble those of too much stomach acid, for which many people take an antacid. But taking antacids would, of course, further reduce stomach acid and make even more nutrients pass through without being absorbed. People with high stomach acid as well as those with low stomach acid may find acid fruit uncomfortable in their stomachs, and avoid orange juice. Low stomach acid can often be the cause of underweight, overweight, constipation, diarrhoea and irritable bowel syndrome, and can lead to more serious illness.

Very often the pancreas, a gland responsible for producing digestive enzymes, as well as for blood sugar balance, will malfunction, either on its own or in sympathy with the stomach. The dominant symptom is a bloated abdomen and diarrhoea or large, soft, offensive stools. Digestive enzyme capsules can be taken, during or immediately preceding a meal, to assist digestion; capsules are better than tablets which take too long to dissolve.

To be healthy it is vital to have a healthy gastro-intestinal tract, which means to have plenty of helpful, friendly bacteria protecting your digestive processes, preventing wind and digestive upsets. When the stomach and pancreas function well, the flora, or bacteria of the small intestine and colon will be healthy and well balanced.

One of the main reasons for dysbiosis, or an imbalance of gut bacteria, is the regular taking of antibiotics for non-life threatening illnesses such as acne and acute bronchitis. When we are babies we receive a colony of bifido bacteria from breast milk, but antibiotics and wrong feeding in subsequent years can soon destroy these delicate organisms. The result is poor digestion, allergies and poor immune function. These bacteria can be replaced but it is important to take 'human strain' bacteria, otherwise they will pass through the gut without building a new colony. There are many cheap acidophilus supplements on the market but they are a false economy; it is important to realise that bifido bacteria for babies, as well as for adults, is fairly expensive. Probiotics, as these bacteria are called (because they colonise the gut rather than decolonise it as antibiotics do), are sometimes prescribed by French and Italian doctors to be taken after a course of antibiotics.

Nowadays many people are sensitive to ordinary everyday foods because of reasons already outlined. This sensitivity may cause almost any symptom or disease – asthma, skin problems such as eczema, aches and pains, weight gain, arthritis or digestive disorders such as IBS. If you have a health problem that you are finding hard to eradicate, try eliminating your favourite food from your diet for three weeks – it could be bread, cheese, chocolate or whatever (but do not stop eating more than one food or you will not be able to identify the culprit). If at the end of three weeks you notice an improvement, you have a sensitivity to that food and would be advised to cut it out of your diet altogether. If you have been vigilant and avoided the appropriate food for three weeks and there is no change, seek the help of a nutritionist to sort out the cause of your condition. Once your health has improved, it is usually possible to reintroduce even those foods to which you were once sensitive.

Vary your diet as much as possible and try not to rely on one food too much. You are not a man-made machine such as a car, running on a diet of four star petrol. And do read all you can about how your body works and how to look after it. It is a sad fact that too many people have more knowledge of their car than of their own body. And remember, too, that doctors are trained in pathology – not in health. They diagnose a pathological condition and then prescribe a drug to try to put that condition right, or at least to attempt to prevent the condition worsening. Anyone who takes a minor problem to a doctor is likely to be told they are wasting surgery time, because doctors are not trained in nutrition or preventative medicine and are only really useful when there is an identifiable mis-function in the body – something to which a label can be attached. So keep your body in a state of constant repair by giving it the right fuel to function properly.

5

Stress Survival Plan

Let's face it: we all come under stress. Sometimes it is 'water off a duck's back', and sometimes we may feel overwhelmed by it. It is when it becomes a permanent feature of life that it damages our physical, mental and emotional health. Stress cannot be waved away as if by magic, but its damaging effects can be drastically reduced. This chapter describes many of the techniques which I have adopted myself and which I have found enormously helpful in managing my own all too frequently stressful life. By dividing them into daily, weekly, fortnightly and occasional techniques I have aimed to address the day-to-day needs of the body as well as to remedy problems which may have accrued over a long period and to guard, in some measure, against future needs.

First Thing

When you get up in the morning run yourself a bath (just below body temperature so that it is slightly invigorating). Just before stepping in add five or six drops of clary sage oil and three drops of geranium, and swish the water very thoroughly to disperse the essential oils evenly. These two oils have a balancing and uplifting effect on the nervous system without being too stimulating, and the geranium, which has a sweet fragrance, blends very well with the 'dry note' of clary sage. Even if it means setting your alarm clock to go off fifteen or twenty minutes earlier it is well worthwhile, as an aromatic bath can impart a note of tranquillity to the start of your day.

If you prefer to shower, as many people do, it will not be possible to incorporate essential oils into your daily cleansing routine, but you can still enjoy the benefits of aromatherapy after your shower. Simply add to a mug of hot water two drops of clary sage and one drop of geranium. Inhale the vapours while you are shaving, applying make-up, doing your hair and so on.

Before dressing, lie on top of your bed for five or ten minutes, and rub a little diluted rose or geranium oil into the solar plexus (see Illustrated Techniques of Application, p. 109). Think about the day ahead and all the things that you have to achieve. Are you worrying about anything? Do you feel any negative emotion such as fear, anxiety or dislike? With your fingertips on your solar plexus, take a deep breath and hold it. Then, as you breathe out, apply gentle pressure to the tender area whilst thinking about your day ahead. Feel the tension disappearing from your abdomen and imagine your negative feelings disappearing also. Continue to do this for a few minutes and then put your arms down by your side and take a few slow, deep breaths. Now tell yourself that you can easily cope with whatever the day is going to bring because you feel strong, calm and in control of your life. When you feel ready to get up, do so slowly.

Dress in colours which enhance you rather than detract from you, as this will give you more confidence. Wearing the right colours really does empower you.

Don't switch on the radio, as the early morning news bulletin is often upsetting and is likely to add to your personal stress. Why do you need to know the sad stories from around the world? If you are having difficulty in handling your own traumas and pressures, it serves no useful purpose for you to take on more sadness. Instead, play a CD or tape of a favourite piece of music. It doesn't need to be slow, meditative music – it can be as fast-paced as you like; but it must make you feel good, and have happy connotations. Beautiful music is soothing to the nerves and could be likened to an auditory massage, so be selective in what you listen to: it is almost as important as what you eat.

Breakfast

First take the following supplements:

- 5 grams vitamin C powder, mixed into water or orange juice.
- One B-complex tablet.
- One evening primrose oil (or other GLA) capsule.
- One multi-vitamin capsule.

As well as the above, if you are very tired because you have had a late night or haven't slept very well, take two guarana capsules or tablets. These will give you sustained energy throughout the day and prevent you having to draw upon nervous energy.

Then eat a proper breakfast. By proper I mean real food such as bread, fruit, porridge, fish, eggs – whatever you fancy, even if it's only one slice of toast and honey with a cup of tea or coffee. But don't eat rubbish such as packets of sweets, jam tarts, sugar-coated breakfast cereals; and no sweet carbonated drinks. These 'sub-foods' create stresses in your body by giving the body excess sugar to handle and making you feel full up, and therefore not able to eat proper food from which your body can repair itself.

Travelling to Work

Traffic jams are an all too common morning event which can create such tension in the muscles of the hands, arms, neck and shoulders that the effects can last all day, causing us to be irritable, more accident-prone and less clear-headed. Very little can be done to avoid rush-hour traffic, but you can make your car a stress-free zone.

Keep a few essential oils in the glove compartment, and when you get stuck in traffic put one or two drops of calming (but not sedative) oil on a tissue. Choose from myrtle, rosewood, bergamot, palmarosa, lemon, grapefruit or orange and waft the tissue under your nose. Do not let any essential oil come into contact with your skin, as they are very concentrated and may cause itching. Alternatively, sprinkle some oils on a corner of your car seat where they cannot come into contact with your clothing.

If listening to the news is adding to your stress, then only play tapes or CDs in your car and really listen to the music instead of treating it as background to your impatient thoughts and concerns about arriving at work on time. It is so easy to shallow-breathe when you are feeling tense, so remember to breathe fully and rhythmically. While you are stuck in traffic use the time to give yourself a hand massage (see Illustrated Techniques of Application, p. 127). In just a few minutes it is possible to unlock from the hands a phenomenal amount of tension which would otherwise travel along your arms into your neck, shoulders and head.

At Work

Commuters are not the only people to experience stress in the mornings. The busy mother coping with the thousand

and one things that have to be done every day for the family has just as hard a time. If you are staying at home, put a few drops of an uplifting, de-stressing oil on to a radiator in winter, or into a bowl of hot water or on an electric or candle fragrancer at other times of year. Choose from orange, lemon, myrtle, patchouli, melissa, verbena, frankincense, lemongrass, rosewood, palmarosa and geranium. Vary the essences so that you do not get too used to any one fragrance. Although essential oils work on an unconscious level by their action in the limbic system, they work even better if you are aware of them. Note how each essence affects you and makes you feel, and use them all with appreciation and gratitude.

If you work in an office, have on your desk a folded tissue impregnated with a drop or two of any one of the above oils, and occasionally pick it up and take a deep breath. You will be surprised at how easy it is to let go of tension when you are inhaling an uplifting yet soothing essential oil. Light oils such as lemon, orange, bergamot and rosewood evaporate quite rapidly, so you will need to refresh the tissue several times throughout the day. Heavier oils such as sandalwood, rose, patchouli and myrtle retain their aromas all day long.

Lunchtime

It's easy to de-stress in a lunch break – before or after you have eaten something nourishing – providing you can find a quiet area in which to sit and relax. If there is nowhere suitable and you feel incredibly tense you might consider the office rest room, if you have one, although this is not ideal. Sit comfortably and place the first and second fingers of both hands on the bump above your eyebrows directly above the inner corner of your eyes (see illustration on page 132). You should be able to feel a pulse under your fingertips. Gently hold this point whilst focusing on your feelings – what has stressed you during the morning, and what further challenges you will have to face in the coming afternoon. You have no need to think further than when you leave for home – it is enough to deal with the immediate past and immediate future. As you hold the forehead points, try to imagine that you are actually touching your stress and that it can leave your head by slipping into your fingertips. Feel the stress flowing into your hands whilst you continue to hold this point. Then lower your arms, stand up slowly and make sure that you wash your hands thoroughly before going back to work. This is very important: the action of washing the hands is not only symbolic of the washing away of stresses, but you can physically wash away vibrations. Ideally you should hold your hands and wrists under running cold water as you wash them.

Afternoon and Early Evening

After work and before driving home or catching the train, take a few minutes to sit quietly. Close your eyes and for a minute or two take some deep breaths. It is incredible to think that normally we only utilise one third of our lungs, and when we panic and shallow-breathe we use even less. If possible, fragrance the immediate space around you so that you are breathing in fresh, revitalising and comforting aromas. Just add a drop or two of an essential oil to a tissue. Lemon or grapefruit are pleasantly refreshing after a busy day, but anyone feeling very tired may prefer to use rosemary or lemongrass as these oils are mentally stimulating – the olfactory equivalent of taking a cold shower. If your job demands have left you with a sick headache at the end of the working day, put a drop of peppermint on to the corner of a tissue and inhale the vapours for a minute or two. Alternatively, keep a packet of peppermint sweets handy. Sucking one of these will release vapours which, when inhaled, will help to relieve a sick headache by relaxing tense stomach muscles.

As with the morning journey, when driving home try to avoid listening to the news and instead play uplifting and emotionally fulfilling music. Control your environment as much as you can; it will enable you to feel more in control of your life. If travelling by train, instead of reading the tabloids and participating in the world's stresses, why not use the journey time to read a humorous book or find out more about one of the alternative therapies described in this book? Bookshops are full of paperbacks on every conceivable aspect of alternative medicine, any one of which could enhance your life.

Let Go of the Day

When you get home, lie on your bed (or on the floor if you prefer) and repeat the morning massage of the solar plexus. Before you lie down, why not fragrance the room with geranium, rose, vetivert, patchouli or any other essential oil which makes you feel relaxed and comfortable?

If your stress is being caused by your job, the people you work with, the building in which you work, or the travelling, then I recommend you take a shower on arriving home. Water is very cleansing, and not only for removing the grime of the day – it will also wash away vibes and bad feelings. Alternatively, run a warm bath and add cleansing and protecting essential oils of rosemary, orange, geranium or palmarosa. If you are planning to go out in the evening, or need to be alert to work from home, then use rosemary, juniper or myrtle in your bath, but if you just want to unwind and do nothing more strenuous than cuddle up to your cats use lavender, neroli or sandalwood.

Now change out of your work clothes. Put on something in which you feel relaxed, in a colour that makes you feel confident and good. If your work obliges you to wear a uniform or a sober suit, you may be wearing colours which deplete your energies and make it more difficult for you to look and feel your best. So it is vital that in the evenings and at weekends you wear colours which are good for you.

Businessmen in particular are often forced to wear grey or blue suits when these colours may not suit them as individuals. It is not possible in this book to go into detail about colour analysis, so I recommend you consult one of the many books on the subject (see Further Reading). But to put it in a nutshell, we can all be categorised as belonging to one of the four seasons – each season has its own colour palette. There are, therefore, good and bad colours for each of us. For example, I am an 'autumn' person and I can wear lots of browns, golds, brown-based reds and pinks, certain greens, neutrals and some yellows. But I cannot wear grey, black or navy blue, nor any blue-based pink or red, because these colours are not part of the autumn palette and don't suit me. The wrong colour can have a negative, even detrimental effect, and now I understand why school was such a place of torture for me – I was forced to wear a navy blue uniform! Colour should enhance us, not detract from us. The right-coloured clothes will always make us feel better because they work in harmony with the colouring of our eyes, skin and hair. Colour analysis with a professional is a worthwhile investment, and I can guarantee that it will enhance your self-confidence and feeling of wellbeing.

Insomniacs have been cured by daily lavender baths, and as this oil is so widely available, inexpensive and gentle in use, it should become an indispensable addition to your bathroom cabinet. Essential oils of lavender, geranium, marjoram, patchouli and linden blossom are all calming and can be used to instill an air of tranquillity in the bedroom. A bedroom can become a haven in which to unwind and sink peacefully into healing sleep.

Finally, don't forget the power of laughter in helping you to unwind. Laughter is a potent medicine and an evening spent at home, whether alone or with a friend/partner, can be very therapeutic if you are able to rent a comedy video. Alternatively, buy yourself a book of jokes. There are bound to be a few that you have not heard before, and you may even find yourself crying with laughter.

Prioritise

Stress tolerance levels can reach breaking point when there is a huge pile of work to take care of, and the list only seems to grow bigger by the day. When mental worry is constantly carried around it robs us of peace and brings us to a point where we feel weighed down by responsibilities. We think. We worry. We feel anxiety. We fear that we can't possibly cope with everything, and yet at the same time we feel afraid that we may have forgotten something important. We can all remember at least one occasion from the past when the magnitude of the work seemed to be too much to bear: swotting for exams; the pile of homework that had to be completed before the end of the school holidays; the dissertation that had to be completed on time; Christmas shopping and present-wrapping that was left until two days before Christmas; pre-wedding planning; moving house and the myriad of detail to be attended to. Whatever it was, we either coped or we didn't. We either just gave up and had a tantrum, muddled through in a bit of a lather, or wrote a list of things to be done and worked our way through it.

I seem to have a permanently long list of things to do, because I lead a rather hectic life with both business and family demands. I have to admit that I have been known to panic – jumping from one task to the other in my desire to get things done. Invariably, I found that I was not quite finishing one job before getting involved with another.

My solution is to take an overview and then to prioritise. I recommend the following procedure to anyone with too much on their plate.

First, brainstorm. Write out a list of everything you have to do – not your daily shower, say, or the cat's feeding time, because these are habitual daily actions that you perform anyway. (But if your neighbour has asked you to feed her cat, and there is a danger that you might forget, write it down on your list.) This is the Big List which you will add to every day. Like a restaurant menu, you will be choosing from this list each day to create your daily Must Do list. When you have finished compiling the Big List and you can clearly see what is being demanded of you – and it may be a hundred and one things – scan through, picking out the six most urgent tasks that have to be done. In order of importance, write the numbers 1–6 next to these tasks. These six are your Must Do list and have to be given priority. Now write them out again on a new piece of paper, this time placing them in order of importance, so that you clearly see that the item at the head of the list has to be tackled first. Then delete these six tasks from the Big List.

Stick the Must Do list where you can regularly refer to it. I use a wall in my study which is near to the door, so that every time I leave the room I can check the list and be reminded of the goals I have set myself for the day. It is so easy to be distracted – the phone rings and you chat for a while, or you suddenly notice that a plant looks thirsty and you water it. A trip to the kitchen for a cup of tea may create another diversion. With a written Must Do list it becomes far easier to refocus your mind on to the urgent tasks that you want to complete. Whatever the interruption, go back to number 1 as soon as you can, and, when it is completed, cross it off the list. Then go on to number 2. If a particular task cannot be completed in a day you should be breaking it down into smaller units – bite-sized pieces – and crossing off each of these when they are completed. If something from the the Big List becomes urgent, delete it from there and add to the Must Do list.

Every day, before going to bed, check through the lists again and write yourself a new Must Do list for the following day.

If you follow this plan, then no matter how many things you have to do and whatever the pressures upon your time you will always be taking care of the most urgent things first. More importantly, however, it will become self-evident as you check over the list and see the crossed off tasks that you are, in fact, coping very well. We often fail to see just how much we have accomplished because we project our thoughts forward. Acknowledging your achievements is a potent form of de-stressing as you not only feel good, but can prove to yourself that you are really in control.

Many people lie awake at night worrying that they may have forgotten something important. Trust that your mind will give you the information you need, and then be ready to 'catch it' with a notebook and pencil. If you remember something important during the night and are not able to recall it in the morning, you will feel very frustrated. Sometimes during the night I wake up with a perfectly clear solution to a problem I have been mulling over during the day. I write it down in my notebook, say 'thank you' and go back to sleep again. If you have a partner who may be disturbed by your note-taking, keep a small torch by your bedside. Also keep a bottle of lavender or marjoram oil by the bed in case you need some help in dropping off to sleep again. Simply put a drop of either oil onto a tissue, or corner of the pillow, and inhale the vapours.

Eat Well Every Day

The Alcohol Fallacy

There's nothing wrong with having a glass or two of wine each day, but if we turn to alcohol to deal with our stress and forget to eat (or lose our desire to eat because drinking is depressing the appetite) then we are actually creating more stress. Stress in any case causes an imbalance in the chemistry of the body, and drinking alcohol only exacerbates the problem.

The adrenal glands, as seen in Chapter 2, take quite a hammering when we are suffering prolonged or severe stress, and they need vitamin C in order to function efficiently. So high stress levels will use up large amounts of vitamin C and in order for us to remain healthy (rather than exist in a 'below par' state) we need to increase our vitamin C intake. But alcohol consumption also makes demands upon the body's vitamin C reserves, so although we may be combating our mental/emotional stress by having a few drinks, unless we take in enough vitamin C each day we are making it more difficult for the adrenal glands to function efficiently, and effectively increasing our physical stress.

Eat Good Food

Even the most expensive bottle of wine or champagne does not contain the nutrients you need to renew and repair body cells. So even if drinking half a bottle a day is part of your lifestyle, do make sure that you eat sensibly, as well as taking 4–5 grams of vitamin C. If you have to travel long distances to and from work, and then set about cooking an evening meal, you may find that you are eating quite late in the evening. But it is always best to eat the main meal of the day at lunchtime or early in the evening. This is because food needs to be partly digested before you go to sleep, and ideally you should be able to leave four hours in between eating and going to bed.

Don't Eat To Combat Stress

Admit what is stressing you. Don't swallow the stress and keep it inside you by continually swallowing more and more food. If you eat because you feel stressed (and not because you are hungry) you are attempting to push down the stress along with the food. So the mere action of eating food will, temporarily, make you feel better. But sooner or later the stress is going to resurface and you will again eat to feel better. This is 'comfort eating', which we have probably all indulged in from time to time. Whilst not particularly harmful during an acute period of stress, if it is allowed to become a chronic habit it will ultimately create other stresses, such as having to spend your hard-earned money on larger clothes because you've grown out of your existing wardrobe. Worse than just damaging your self-esteem and finances, there is a real danger that it could affect your future health by putting undue strain on your heart, kidneys and liver.

Exercise On a Regular Basis

It doesn't have to be much – twenty minutes a day of something simple like skipping with a rope, or using a stepping machine, is quite enough. Even trotting up and down stairs several times a day is highly beneficial, as is taking a brisk walk to the bus stop or corner shop. What we need is something which forces us to breathe a little faster. When we exercise we are not only keeping the muscles of our body in good order but, far more importantly, we are exercising the muscles of the heart. This is very important if we want to remain healthy and avoid heart trouble in later life – and cope with the stresses of day-to-day living.

It's never too late to take up the habit of exercise, as long as you bear in mind that the body needs to build up its strength gradually so that you don't overstrain anything. So only gentle exercise should be taken at first. Build up your stamina and only push yourself a little beyond what feels comfortable. You will come to find, over the course of days and weeks, that you are able to increase your exercise time without experiencing any discomfort. Walking is a particularly good and cheap form of exercise and can be a pleasant and uplifting activity, especially if you live in the country, near to the coast or have access to a park or river bank.

One of the best forms of exercise for de-stressing the mind as well as the body is tai chi chuan, an ancient Chinese discipline. Tai chi is one of the classical martial arts, and when practised regularly and long term, is a potent form of self-defence. But even for the laziest and most un-exercised of persons, tai chi is a very gentle and easy-to-follow form of exercise, being both relaxing and graceful. An introductory video is an ideal way to acquaint yourself with 'shortform' tai chi which is recommended for beginners (see Further Reading).

Once a Week

Just once a week (or more often if you feel it necessary) write an angry letter. Say anything and everything you want to say to whoever it is that is upsetting you. It can be your noisy neighbour; the traffic warden who gave you a ticket even though you were standing at the cash-point machine whilst he wrote it out; your errant child; a teacher from your past – the one who made you feel stupid in front of the whole class; your boss who doesn't appreciate your efforts; your least favourite politician who has been quoted, once again, talking absolute twaddle. It doesn't really matter who the letter is to or what their address is, because you won't be sending the letter. This is a get-it-off-your-chest letter, and for your eyes only. Read it through and imagine the effect it is having on the recipient. Whether you choose to file it or destroy it is a personal choice, but I sometimes like to tear it up into tiny pieces or ceremoniously burn it. If you don't have an open fire indoors or a suitable area in your garden, the kitchen sink is always a good place to burn a piece of paper.

Once you have vented your anger, you need to defuse any residual anger left in you. The best way to do so is to show some love to yourself. Try rubbing scented oils into your shoulders, neck, arms or legs. It is almost impossible to stay cross whilst you are massaging fragrantly soothing oils into your skin. Or take a long, languorous bath scented with your favourite essences. Particularly effective at releasing anger are ylang-ylang, geranium, rose, clary sage and chamomile. Promise yourself a nightly face massage – it need not take longer than five minutes and is simple to prepare. To one or two teaspoons of sweet almond oil or similarly good fatty oil add two or three drops of any of the following: melissa, rose, neroli, geranium, palmarosa, bergamot or ylang-ylang.

If massage does not appeal to you or you have a lot of energy which needs to be channelled, do something physical. Go swimming, step exercising, skipping, yoga, tai chi, jogging on the spot or whatever you feel like. And don't forget that sexual intercourse with your partner is a very good form of exercise as well as being a wonderful way of letting go of tension. Too much stress can reduce your libido and sexual response, but this can often be remedied with aromatherapy, (see 'sexual problems' in A-Z section).

Once A Fortnight

Have a fortnightly massage, either from a professional aromatherapist or from a friend/partner. During a stressful two-week period we can store up an incredible amount of tension in the muscles of the upper back, shoulders and neck, and if this tension is not released it can create many problems – headaches, inability to sleep, forgetfulness, irritability and a general feeling of malaise. Massage of the back, neck and shoulders (see Illustrated Techniques) can unlock tight muscles, allowing stored memories to leave the body. When this tension is released there is a perceptible lightening of the load, which is why clients walk out of a treatment session feeling as though they are walking on air. But even without going to a professional aromatherapist, a massage with essential oils, when given with love, can take away an incredible amount of stress and replace it with a wonderful sense of well-being.

Occasionally

Every so often write a forgiving letter. After having written a few angry letters and released a lot of pent-up emotion – the emotion of anger – it is equally valuable to let go of hatred and resentment, either of which, if allowed to stew inside you, could become the precipitating factor in a serious disease. It may well be impossible for you to express forgiveness in a face-to-face situation because that person is too far away, no longer alive or wouldn't want to see you. The important thing is to feel yourself expressing forgiveness to someone who has wronged you.

The easiest way to express yourself may be to speak aloud when you are alone in your room and there is no one to question your motives or cause you embarrassment. Or perhaps you are best able to express yourself by writing a forgiving letter. As with the angry letter, there is no need to post the letter of forgiveness. It is enough that you have, with sincerity, let go of a deep-held hurt. Don't be surprised if you feel upset or even burst into tears. This is a healthy, natural process, helping to wash away the negativity you have been holding on to for so long.

Afterwards, have a long, fragrant soak in your bath and then go to bed. Use your favourite essential oil or choose from lavender, myrtle, rosewood, frankincense, clary sage, geranium or ylang-ylang. If it is not convenient to take a bath, add a few drops of any of the above oils to a fragrancer or bowl of hot water and lie down quietly for half an hour.

Instead of Worrying, Have a Contingency Plan

With the increasing unpredictability of the weather, politics and the financial market, many people feel anxious about the future. Their fear is not unfounded – as stocks and shares take a tumble, nobody seems very sure about the future of Europe, and global weather patterns have become more and more erratic, with flooding a regular matter of major concern. Yet to spend time worrying about what may happen is not going to alter things. Worry only increases stress levels and creates more unhappiness and disharmony. Instead of worrying about the future, I believe it is better to take a few practical steps to shield yourself against unforeseen circumstances. You don't have to be a survivalist in order to plan ahead: it is common practice among government departments, hospitals and many other public institutions, so that in the event of an emergency there are resources at hand which can be called upon until the status quo is restored. So gather together a few basic provisions to give you a little extra peace of mind.

All human beings need, in order of importance, water, food and medicine. Pets require the same. My recommendation is to buy in a large bag of rice, a few litres of bottled water and some cans of food (vegetables and your favourite canned meat, fish or whatever). Check the 'use by' date on the packs and tins to make sure they are not old stock, so that you have several months at least before they need to be used up. Also get in a supply of pet food, if appropriate. You'll need several other camping-type pieces of equipment, such as a can opener, candles, matches, plasters, a small selection of bandages, a torch with spare batteries and bulbs, and possibly a small camping stove and spare gas bottle in the event of mains gas and electricity supplies being disrupted. Find a suitable storage place for your provisions and don't be tempted to use them simply because you haven't had time to go shopping (but if you do, replace them within a few days). Make a note of the 'use by' dates in a small notebook, and check it once a month. Anything which is approaching its date should be consumed and a replacement obtained. If you do this, then none of the provisions will ever go to waste, and even if they are never needed in an emergency situation you have not wasted any money.

Emergency medicines can be kept very simple with just a few homeopathic remedies and a small selection of essential oils. I recommend a bottle of arnica tablets (in the sixth potency), as arnica is superb at lessening shock and relieving the ache of over-used muscles. If kept in its original sealed container this remedy will retain its potency for several years. There are several other homeopathic remedies which are ideal for an emergency first aid kit, but they need to be used in conjunction with a reference book (see Further Reading).

Essential oils should be stored in a separate container to the homeopathic remedies. Sunlight and oxygen are enemies of essential oils, and the delicate homeopathic remedies can be antidoted by any of the camphoraceous essential oils. Properly stored, however, both types of medicine will keep for a considerable time.

Obtain a few bottles of those essential oils which have first aid properties – oils which are styptic (to stem the flow of blood), antiseptic and skin repairing (for wounds), healing to burns, and which neutralise the poison of insect stings and bites. Two essential oils fulfil all these requirements: lavender and tea tree, both of which are inexpensive and widely available in high street chemists, health food stores and elsewhere. A third essence which I consider a valuable addition to a medicine chest is ravansara, an anti-viral essential oil that is capable of aborting a cold or flu if used at the onset of infection. Lemon oil may be added to the collection, as it can be added to water if there is a danger of waterborne contamination. There is no guarantee that lemon oil will neutralise all pathogens, but it does have the power to inhibit the growth of many bacteria. (When travelling in India, I have stayed healthy and free from diarrhoea by adding five drops of lemon oil to every 500ml of bottled water. Even when drinking only bottled water, it is impossible to travel in India without ingesting airborne bacteria).

Honey can be classed as a medicine as well as a food, and a few jars of organic runny honey are a good investment as they can be stored indefinitely and have a myriad of uses. It is antibacterial and has for centuries been used for healing wounds. (Even deep wounds which cannot be stitched for fear of infection developing deep in the tissues have been known to heal, without leaving any scar tissue, when treated with organic honey.) Honey is also a natural laxative (though not a purgative) and can help to normalise stools after a period of constipation. Being easily assimilated into the bloodstream, honey will give instant energy if you eat one or two teaspoons of it.

Insurance company advertisements often talk about their policies bringing 'peace of mind' and allude to them as being 'as strong as castle walls', protecting the people within. But there are limits to their usefulness. Insurance companies will (to one degree or another) reimburse the client who has lost possessions in a flood, fire and so on, but no policy is going to supply you with food and water should a landslide, earthquake or flood temporarily cut you off from the rest of civilisation. Extra insurance will never give you the peace of mind that you will receive from practical contingency planning. So be prudent: plan ahead, and then stop worrying about what might happen. There are enough stresses to cope with in your day-to-day existence without projecting your thoughts into the future. So appreciate the life you have now and live every day as it comes.

6

Other Alternatives

- Acupuncture
- Applied kinesiology
- Bach flower remedies
- Cranio-sacral therapy
- Homeopathy
- Hypnotherapy
- McTimony chiropractic
- NLP (neuro-linguistic programming)
- Psychotherapy
- Reflexology
- Shiatsu
- Vitamin therapy

Aromatherapy can help many different problems, but if you need help with a specific health problem it may be better used in conjunction with another appropriate therapy. Certainly the use of essential oils will improve your wellbeing, but some conditions require additional help.

This chapter outlines the main points of the twelve alternative therapies listed above. There are of course many others, such as osteopathy and herbal medicine, which may be equally good in the treatment of stress and stress-related conditions, but I have chosen this particular assortment because I have experienced all these therapies at some time or another and know their benefits.

The type of therapy you seek will depend upon the stress-related condition from which you are suffering. The majority are 'hands on', such as McTimony chiro-practic and cranio-sacral therapy which are particularly suited to treating stress-related problems caused by physical and structural imbalances – lower back pain and tension headaches are two examples. Other 'hands on' therapies include applied kinesiology, shiatsu, reflex-ology and acupuncture. Therapies which enable a person to let go of stored trauma and stress by talking about it include NLP, hypnotherapy and psychotherapy, whilst remedies which are ingested include homeopathy and Bach flower remedies (both of which particularly benefit emotional stress) and vitamin therapy.

To make it easier to contact a practitioner whose therapy is most appropriate to your needs I have included the names and telephone numbers of each of the therapists who so kindly contributed to this chapter (see Useful Addresses, p. 255). Contact information for the national association of each of the therapies is also included.

Acupuncture

A system which is thousands of years old, acupuncture is part of oriental medicine which includes herbalism, diet, exercise and manipulation. The basic premise in acupunc-ture is that each organ (for instance, the lungs) relates to a channel or meridian along which the life-force or chi energy flows. There are fourteen major meridians and each one has a specific number of acupuncture points at precise locations along its pathway. These points are stimulated in one of several ways – by acupuncture needles, the use of a warming herb known as moxa, or via pressure as in acupressure or shiatsu. Dis-ease is seen to be an imbalance in the life-force – either excess or deficiency – which the practitioner seeks to redress.

Understanding and differentiating the types of stress is not specific to oriental medicine but is an intergral part of acupuncture treatment. Oriental medicine holds that disease has either an internal or an external cause. External causes are exposure to damp, wind, heat, cold, dryness and so on, any one of which can have an invasive effect. For example, sitting on a damp lawn may lead to getting a chill, or sitting in a draught may produce a stiff neck. Other factors would be poor diet, overwork and other lifestyle-related problems.

Internal causes are concerned with emotional imbalances. Each organ/meridian is linked to specific emotions, for instance the lungs with grief, so an excess of grief is said to be injurious to the lungs. Acupuncture can be helpful in cases where a patient has difficulty in coming to terms with loss or bereavement.

Each person who shows symptoms of stress is said to have a primary imbalance in one particular meridian – either a constitutional imbalance or one acquired before the age of seven. A practitioner would assess this imbalance and treat it accordingly. Acupunture can be very relaxing and therefore enable the patient to cope more effectively with stress, as well as dealing with the underlying causes of the problem.

Applied Kinesiology

This is a system of diagnosis and treatment which grew out of chiropractic medicine (see p. 86) in the early 1960s. The basic idea is that certain muscles relate to particular organs – hence their related acupuncture meridians. Associated with each muscle are a number of reflexes which stimulate temperature and blood supply. It is an extremely powerful diagnostic system which can ascertain a person's nutritional requirements as well as refine any structural examination.

In AK there are said to be four types of stress: physical, chemical, thermal and emotional. Physical stress includes long working hours, physical exertion, lack of sleep and mechanical strain due to injury or bad postural habits. Chemical stress includes poor diet, excess intake of additives, pollution, medication, the use of alcohol, tobacco and so-called recreational drugs. Great emphasis is placed on the role of low blood sugar (hypoglycemia) and adrenal fatigue (hypoadrenia). Thermal stress is caused either by overheating or excess chilling. This would apply, for instance, to people working in hothouses or refrigerated areas. This can adversely affect the adrenals and, in acupuncture terms, the triple heater, which acts as the body's thermostat.

The last category is that of emotional stress. This can be a difficult area to treat because it requires the patient to make changes in lifestyle, attitudes and emotional habits. Stress is cumulative, and a person can have mild stress in several of these categories or be particularly stressed in only one area.

A simple method of alleviating stress is to place the pads of the fingers on the bumps of the forehead (the frontal prominences) and to feel for a pulse. Quietly hold these until the pulses synchronise, which may take a minute or two or even longer if the stress is very intense. This technique has been proven to calm the mind of someone under stress because it can allow heat and tension, which builds up inside the head during times of stress, to dissipate. Whilst this technique is being used the person can be encouraged to think about past, future or present stresses. Bringing these stressful thoughts to the attention of the conscious mind at this time is extremely relaxing and can quickly bring about a more detached state of mind.

Bach Flower Remedies

The remedies used are all prepared from the flowers of wild plants, bushes and trees, and none of them is harmful or habit-forming. They were discovered by a doctor who had practised for over twenty years in London as a Harley Street consultant, bacteriologist and homeopath. The late Edward Bach, MB, BS, MRCS, LRCP, DPH gave up his lucrative practice in 1930 to devote all his energies to the plant world. His aim was to restore vitality to sick people, so that they themselves would be able to overcome their worry, apprehension and so on and thus assist in their own healing.

Dr Bach developed great sensitivity in both mind and body. If he held his hand over a flowering plant, or held the flower in the palm of his hand, he could sense the properties of that flower. Before finding a particular flower he would suffer in himself, and very acutely, the negative state of mind for which that flower was needed; at the same time, he was privileged, as he said, to suffer from some physical complaint. Then he would wander about the fields and lanes until he was 'led' to the flowers which would immediately restore his serenity and peace of mind. Within a few hours the physical complaint would also be healed.

Bach flower remedies are used, not directly for physical complaints, but for the sufferer's worry, apprehension, hopelessness, irritability and so on. These states of mind or moods not only hinder the recovery of health and retard convalescence, but are generally accepted as primary causes of sickness and disease.

A long-held worry or fear will deplete the individual's vitality; he will feel out of sorts and the body then loses its natural resistance. But as peace and harmony are achieved unity returns to mind and body – closing the circuit, as it were, and allowing the life-force to flow freely again, thus giving the body a chance to produce its own natural healing.

Dr Bach found that thirty-eight flowers covered all the known negative states of mind from which mankind can suffer, categorising them under seven headings:

● Apprehension.
● Uncertainty and indecision.
● Loneliness.
● Insufficient interest in present circumstances.
● Oversensitivity to ideas and influences.
● Despondency and despair.
● Too much care for the welfare of others.

Alternatively, make up a 30 ml (1fl. oz) bottle filled with spring water and one teaspoon brandy (as a preservative) and add the chosen drops. The dose is four drops taken directly on the tongue and repeated at least four times a day.

This system of treatment is very easy to understand and follow, making it quite simple for sufferers to help themselves as well as others. It can be used with impunity to help children, teenagers, adults, pregnant and nursing mothers and the elderly, and can be used in conjunction with other alternative therapies.

Bach Flower Remedies *do not* require a practitioner as Dr Bach intended for us to recognise our own negative traits and then to actively seek to transform them to positive. However, a book is necessary to help you pinpoint which of the thirty-eight remedies are applicable to you (see Further Reading).

Cranio-sacral Therapy

This therapy has the great advantage that it is suitable for people of all ages from babies to the elderly. Being extremely gentle, it is eminently suitable for even acutely painful ailments and is capable of helping a variety of health problems whether physically or emotionally based.

From the moment we are born, stress is a part of life. Even before the moment of birth a baby's skull is compressed as it is squeezed through the narrow birth canal. When it emerges, the bones move into their correct position and should slide against each other in a rhythmic movement. If this does not happen, the pressure in the skull can cause headaches, dyslexia and other learning and behavioural difficulties. By checking a baby's skull within the first few days, and then occasionally throughout the first year of life, the stress of birth can be released and future problems prevented.

As we grow older the stresses increase, building tension within the body. It is now known that muscles have a memory, and can store both physical and emotional trauma. As the neck muscles tense they restrict the blood flow and consequently the oxygen to the brain, causing headaches, concentration problems, lethargy, sleeping difficulties and, in some cases, menstrual problems if the pituitary gland is affected. Similarly tense muscles elsewhere can cause asthma, sciatica and arthritis.

What is called the cranio-sacral rhythm flows throughout the body. It is a result of the skull and spine expanding and contracting as the cerebro-spinal fluid, which protects the brain and nerves, flows in and out. By tuning into this rhythm it is possible for the therapist to assess any strain, restriction or injury, whether recent or longstanding, throughout the body.

Having diagnosed an abnormality it can then be very gently released, working with the body's natural desire to self-heal. As the rhythm is re-established, an overall sense of wellbeing is experienced. A session is usually extremely relaxing, lasts forty-five minutes and involves lying on a couch in loose-fitting, lightweight clothing.

There are some examples of the effects of cranio-sacral therapy:– a severely stressed executive found that after only two sessions he was sleeping better, was able to turn his neck freely, had lost his evening headaches and was able to eat without any pain in his jaw; having suffered severe family problems, a mother was plagued by constant headaches for three months after the trauma had stopped. She obtained total relief from pain after only one session – releasing her stiff neck had relieved the pressure on her skull; finally, physical stress, such as that of whiplash in a car crash, can injure the delicate structure of the neck and cause headaches and neck pain. Craniosacral work is so effective that even long-standing cases have been successfully treated in only two or three sessions.

Homeopathy

In homeopathy stress is viewed as a causative factor in many illnesses. Do you remember when you took your exams, moved house, prepared for a major event, worried about someone or simply overworked? A cold or flu may have come on, or headaches, or tiredness. This was your body telling you to stop because you were overdoing things. You may have listened and slowed down or made changes to your lifestyle, and soon got better. But all too often the message is not understood, and the symptoms are either ignored or else suppressed with stimulants or painkillers. Sadly, in many cases this leads to deeper, more troublesome ailments and finally to chronic disease. Homeopathy can nip such developments in the bud and can reverse the downhill trend, even if the condition has become chronic. Many people with conditions that are conventionally regarded as incurable have responded well to homeopathic treatment.

Homeopathy has been used for over two hundred years and is based on Samuel Hahnemann's rediscovery of the way of treatment by 'similars' as an alternative to the conventional treatment with 'opposites'. In homeopathy the whole person is treated and the disease is seen as a result of the body's inability to adapt to change. Each person is a unique individual with different needs, abil-

ities, tastes, susceptibilities and constitutions. The homeopathic remedies are selected accordingly, by matching the
symptom picture of the patient with that of a 'similar'
remedy. The 'similar' remedy is one that, taken by a
healthy person, would cause symptoms and sensations
like those experienced by the sufferer. These symptoms
are recorded in minute detail in the homeopaths' reference
works, known as the Repertories and Materia Medicas.

In homeopathy much attention is given to 'exciting'
causes and 'maintaining' causes: in other words, what
may have brought on the disease (the exciting cause) and
what stops it from disappearing (the maintaining cause).
Stress is often found to be the exciting cause, the maintaining cause or both. Here are some examples.

Case 1: Stress as the 'Exciting' Cause

A forty-one-year-old woman lost her mother and sister in
a car accident a year ago. Since then her periods have
been very erratic, her appetite is so diminished that she
has to force herself to eat and she dissolves in tears at the
slightest offence. Her family and friends are very supportive, but her father suffered a stroke as a result of the
shock and needs constant care and attention. Her energy
is low and she worries terribly that something else might
happen. Her stomach feels tight like a knot. When she
sleeps, she often dreams of her dead relatives. She sighed
often during the homeopathic interview.

The remedy ignatia was given in a medium high potency, one dose to be taken at first. Its beneficial effect
was felt almost immediately in the way she felt about life
and in her appetite returning. Her husband remarked on
how she was regaining her strength, coping better and
crying less often. She was given a few doses of ignatia to
keep and to take when she felt it was necessary. At the
next consultation one month later she was much improved, and her period had arrived on time. She had
only needed to repeat the ignatia once, after an upsetting

visit to her father. She has come to terms with the tragedies in her life and coped remarkably well with the challenges that were to follow.

Case 2: Stress as the 'Maintaining' Cause

A sixteen-year-old girl is due to take her GCSE exams in a few months' time. She has been diagnosed as having glandular fever. She is under a lot of stress at school, with pressure to participate in extra-school activities. She has a disabled older sister and a younger brother and very supportive parents. She is popular with everybody, the sunshine of the family, who always copes and hardly ever complains. But her body shows that all is not well. She finds going to sleep difficult, easily tires from any physical exertion and suffers from headaches and great thirst. The glands in her neck swell up occasionally.

Her constitutional remedy was worked out and given daily in liquid form for a few months, during which time things gradually improved. Changes in her lifestyle were discussed too, and the stress reduced by cutting out some of her extra-curricular activities. She did well in her exams and fully recovered from the glandular fever.

Homeopathy is widely used in Britain and can at present be studied and practised by anybody. It is advisable to choose a practitioner either by personal recommendation or by contacting one of the organisations listed at the back of the book. Homeopathy is easy to learn, and self-help courses are available from most local evening classes.

McTimony Chiropractic

Many people who attend for McTimony chiropractic treatment are seeking relief from physical symptoms which may have resulted from, or be contributing to, various forms of stress. By gently realigning the skeleton, and particularly the spinal column, the McTimony chiropractor aims to remove distortion or interference of the nervous system and calm the stress response.

Chiropractors are concerned with the structural relationship between nerve tissue and the spinal column which houses and protects those tissues. As long as the individual bones or vertebrae of the spine remain correctly aligned, the nerve pathways of the spinal cord and the nerve roots which branch out along its length will be protected and function correctly. However, one or more of the vertebrae often become misaligned. This is called a 'subluxation' of the bone and can interfere with the healthy operation of the nervous system at that point.

Subluxations are often implicated in stress. Accidents can displace the vertebrae either by a direct hit on the bone or from a sudden shock to the system. Where, for example, a fall in childhood produces subluxations, symptoms may not appear for many years. The inexplicable chronic pain that eventually occurs could become a source of stress in later life. In this case, chiropractic care could correct the subluxation and bring relief from the symptoms which have produced the stress.

Subluxation can also result directly from stress. Abnormal muscle tension and posture will produce subluxations that can themselves be the source of further symptoms, contributing to general stress levels. Perhaps someone experiences anxiety stemming from financial problems; this generates tension in the neck and shoulders as they 'bear the burden' of working or looking after house and family. The neck tension causes subluxations which affect the nerves supplying muscles in the arms. This reduces coordination, making the person accident prone, or produces numbness and pins and needles in the hands, creating more stress – and so on. Chiropractic treatment can help to break the cycle of stress symptoms, allowing an opportunity to review the situation and make positive changes to deal with the original cause of anxiety. Many of the symptoms of stress indicate that our body is in conflict with itself through an over-stimulated nervous system.

During a McTimony chiropractic treatment the chiropractor will check and carefully adjust the bones of the skull, spine, pelvis and limbs, relieving subluxations throughout the body. Once distortions of the nervous system are removed, the body can begin to function correctly once again. People undergoing McTimony chiropractic often report improvements in sleep patterns, digestive problems or period pains, as well as finding relief from the more structural aches and pains that prompted them to seek treatment.

One noticeable feature of the McTimony technique for those suffering from stress is its gentleness. Many people comment on how relaxed they feel during the treatment, and this in itself is very beneficial.

NLP – Neuro-linguistic Programming

NLP is a proven way of looking at our stresses, worries and perceived problems and, after forming a mental picture of those stresses, playing with them in such a way as to become the controller of those stressors instead of those stresses controlling us. Since its development by John Ginder and Richard Bandler in the USA some years ago, NLP has expanded into a considerable body of knowledge – skills and techniques which can help people in almost any area of their lives. Applications range from health and personal difficulties to business management problems.

The easiest way to understand the way NLP works is to experience it for yourself, which can be easily done. As you are reading this book, you are aware of yourself; aware of what you can see and hear around you; and aware of what you can feel touching your body – perhaps your back against a chair. You are also aware of your own 'inner world' – what your feelings and thoughts are; you may see pictures inside your head of what happened yesterday or what you expect to happen tomorow; you may hear yourself 'replaying' the past or rehearsing for the future; you may be re-experiencing the feelings of an event from the past or having feelings of anticipation for the future.

For the moment, just notice for about sixty seconds what aspects of the previous paragraph apply to you. Neuro-linguistic programming as a discipline works with your 'map of the world'. This map is unique to you and is created by you, using your own senses – that is, what you see, what you hear, what you smell, what you taste and what you feel through your nervous system, and how you interpret these experiences through your own values, beliefs and rules. Your nervous system is unique to you and how you choose to use it – in other words, communicate to youself and others. It is as vital a tool of communication as language.

What stresses you now may not stress others and, indeed, may not have stressed you in the past and may not stress you in the future. Look up from reading and select something which has caused you minor stress in the past. Do you see a picture in your mind's eye? If so, where is that picture? In front of you in close-up, or far away? Is it in colour or black and white? If it is close then move it further away, and if it is far away bring the image closer to you. If large, make it tiny or do the very opposite. If in colour, change it to black and white and then back again to colour. Notice each time you make changes how you feel. Do you feel less stressful or more so? Then do the same for your other senses too. For example, if a voice is harsh and close, make it calm and only as close as is comfortable for you. Choose how to respond to events rather than letting them stress you. By repeating these simple exercises you can expand your area of choice and find what works for you.

Psychotherapy and Hypnotherapy

The term 'psychotherapy' is often used in a wide sense to include virtually any therapy which treats the psyche (literally 'soul'; more usually, 'mind'; or even 'inner self'. More specifically – and usefully – it would refer only to that group of therapies which recognise and try to work with the unconscious mind. This is where psychotherapy would differ from, say, counselling, which deliberately restricts itself to the conscious here-and-now of the client's situation. Both approaches overlap – you can't really use psychotherapy without using counselling skills – but the psychotherapist will also look for clues in, and help from, that hinterland of the mind which reveals itself in a number of unintended and uncontrolled ways. The most obvious of these would be dreams, although there are a number of other ways of producing and utilising unconscious material.

Whatever form it takes, treatment will consist mainly, or entirely, of talking. A lot of this will be about how present problems have their patterns in the past – most of us carry too much emotional baggage around with us and very often don't realise how strong a hold it has, precisely because so much of it is unconscious. Freedom from this creates a real change of attitude in the client towards him/herself and, often, towards the world. This is a freedom which begets more freedom – which is the object of the exercise.

It is difficult to answer one of the first questions that every client asks: 'How many sessions will it take?' It is possible for a client to respond remarkably in half a dozen. Then again, it may be that a client will need to attend sessions for two or three years. The average length of treatment is probably about fifteen sessions, but it varies enormously from client to client and from therapist to therapist.

Hypnotherapy is sometimes used in conjunction with psychotherapy as this dual approach can considerably shorten the treatment time. Unfortunately, the appeal of hypnotherapy is too often based on misconceptions fostered by theatrical performances which give the impression that the hypnotist has some sort of magical power. Not surprisingly, this creates in many people a false hope that a therapist who uses hypnosis will be able to magic their problems away, possibly in one session and with little or no effort from the client. In reality, all therapy is hard work because you can't cheat nature, and real therapy is always natural. Having said that, hypnosis – which may be defined as the induction and utilisation of trance states – can be a very helpful tool, because the trance state is natural and can be used in a number of ways. To take just one instance, someone in trance may well have better access to repressed emotions and also, being in a suggestible state, be more open to ideas which have a releasing effect on them.

It is true that some conditions can be treated quickly if there is no real depth to them. If all you want, say, is to stop smoking, then a quick 'fix' may well suffice. But if, as so often happens, your problem is saying something about your whole life, then you need someone who knows how to practise psychotherapy, whether or not hypnosis is used as a part of the treatment.

Reflexology

Although reflexology has been practised for more than five thousand years, it is only during the last decade or so that it has become a popular alternative therapy. It is based on the principle that running the length of the body are ten zones: five on either side, ending in each foot and extending into the fingertips. Energy is constantly flowing through these zones. On each hand or foot are reflex points which correspond with every organ and gland of the body.

Stimulating or working any zone by applying pressure with thumb and fingers affects the entire zone throughout the body. Any sensitive area on the foot would mean that there is congestion in that organ or body part which in turn can affect other organs in that zone as the flow of energy is impaired by the blockage. Crystals can also form near joints; these deposits are formed by uric acid and calcium, which is drawn down by gravity into the foot. When such a blockage occurs it indicates where a problem lies, and the aim of reflexology is to break down these crystals to allow the energy to flow and to encourage the body systems to work again in unison.

Reflexology alleviates the effects of stress by inducing deep, tranquil relaxation – you can even fall asleep during a treatment. We have more than seven thousand nerves in our feet, and by stimulating them it enables messages to reach our spinal cord and brain. Information is then relayed to the organs and muscles which have been impaired by stress, with the consequence that the messages which were being delivered slowly, unreliably or not at all begin to get through at the correct speed.

Stress tightens up the cardiovascular system and restricts blood-flow. With restricted blood-flow there is an impediment in the body's attempts to carry oxygen and nutrients to all the cells that make up the tissues of the body. The flow of waste matter is also restricted, resulting in toxic matter remaining in the body for unhealthily long periods. This will, in time, cause problems such as headaches, earache, high blood pressure, backache and many more minor ailments. The organs of the elimination system – the lymph nodes, kidneys, colon and skin – can become blocked with toxins and waste matter builds up. As a result our body starts to feel sluggish and lethargic, which can easily precipitate the early stages of disease. Reflexology helps these systems to function more efficiently, and rebalances the body so that natural self-healing can take place.

Reflexology can help to detect problems before they appear in the body, and is a useful preventative medicine for catching early warning signs as well as for treatment of disorders by natural means. It not only relaxes the whole body but also the mind, and is thus an invaluable therapy for the elimination of tension and stress.

Shiatsu

This is a Japanese healing technique closely related to acupuncture. Shiatsu literally means 'finger pressure', which describes the fundamental technique, although in its complete application it involves a practitioner using their thumbs, fingers and palms on specific energy channels (meridians) and points (tsubos) of a recipient, combined with gentle stretches and rotations of the limbs.

Receiving shiatsu enables one to relax deeply, to strengthen where there is weakness and to release where there is tension and stiffness. Relief from both long- and short-term physical and emotional problems can be gained, encouraging vitality, flexibility, improved circulation and overall wellbeing.

The stress that quickly accumulates in the mind and body can easily be relieved by the deeply effective touch of shiatsu. Caring support, combined with active application of pressure to specific points throughout the body, enables the circulation of energy, blood and the lymphatic system to flow with greater strength and effectiveness. All these body functions are affected by stress, and thus benefit greatly from shiatsu, which also relieves areas that have become stiff, aching and tired from the effects of stress. This facilitates the softening and opening of the joints and ligaments, and the relaxation of the internal organs.

Although shiatsu may appear to be a very simple technique, we must not forget that it draws on an understanding of the vastly complex and historic system of oriental medicine, combined with the subtle and sensitive touch of the practitioner. It is this very fundamental technique of touch that could be said to bring the greatest of all relief from stress and subsequent health disorders and disease, enabling us to manage stressful environments and situations with greater ease.

Vitamin Therapy

This form of therapy also incorporates the use of minerals, as a body under stress uses up a phenomenal amount of these nutrients. Nowadays, more than at any time in the past, it is vital to supplement our diet with vitamins and minerals in order to protect ourselves from stress and pollution. But there are dozens of vitamin and mineral products available, and to wander into a high street store without knowing which to buy could in itself prove to be stressful. Within the wide choice, there is also a huge discrepancy in the formulation of supplements – some are easily assimilated, whilst others require a fully competent digestive system in order to break them down, before they can begin to be used by the body. Our bodies need vitamins and minerals in varying amounts and, although many are to be found in small quantities in the food we eat, others are so crucial to the efficient functioning of our bodies that we really need to take higher doses than we can obtain from our daily intake of food. Below is a summary of the key nutrients required by our bodies.

Vitamin C

This is probably the most important vitamin for the treatment of stress. It improves adrenal hormone output, helps to normalise blood sugar metabolism and prevents scurvy. The average person lives just below the scurvy level – in fact the Recommended Daily Allowance (RDA) for vitamin C used to be 30mg which would just about prevent the condition. Symptoms of this age-old disease are weakness, lethargy, easy bruising, bleeding gums, loosening teeth, pains in joints and internal haemorrhaging. If unchecked, the result is death.

Don't imagine that drinking orange juice every day will provide you with enough vitamin C. A gorilla roaming free will consume 14g a day of the vitamin in fruits and leaves to keep himself in peak condition, and if we relate that to human body size then we probably need 7–9g a day (7000–9000mg). An orange contains 50mg and the average 100ml glass of orange juice contains 35mg.

It is best to take vitamin C as it occurs in fruits and vegetable, which is known as magnesium ascorbate and is the kind preferred by nutritionists, who understand about the absorption of nutrients (See Recommended Supplement Regime on p. 252).

Vitamin B

The vitamins of the B complex are known to be anti-stress nutrients. They are also involved in sugar balance in the blood, in protecting the adrenal glands and in helping to keep our skin and hair healthy.

Vitamin B6 regulates the balance between sodium and potassium in the body. It is tremendously important to all body functions, including hormone function. Deficiency can cause obesity, a serious lack of energy and damage to the pancreas. Dosage: 25–50mg a day of Pyridoxol 5 phosphate (Biocare or Solgar).

B5 or pantothenic acid is primarily an anti-stress factor, as it feeds and stimulates the adrenal glands. Its use is important to prevent menopausal symptoms, and it is helpful in gout and arthritis. Deficiency can cause hypoglycemia (low blood sugar) and low blood pressure. Dosage: 50mg–1500mg a day.

Vitamin E

This vitamin improves the oxygenation of cells. It is one of the antioxidant family, helping to prevent damage by free radicals as a result of pollution, altered fats (see Chapter 4) and sunshine. It is helpful in dealing with hot flushes, and should therefore be taken during and leading up to the menopause. Dosage: 100–600iu, (international unit) a day, building up gradually.

Zinc (Zn)

This mineral is essential for the endocrine system so as to ensure balanced hormonal output, and is vital for healthy reproduction and nearly every metabolic action in the body. For instance, the liver uses zinc to metabolise alcohol, after which the zinc is excreted in urine. It is a very good idea, when planning a pregnancy, for both partners to avoid alcohol as much as possible for the preceding three months. This will ensure both healthy egg and sperm. Deficiency of zinc can lead to acne, anorexia nervosa, allergies, poor liver function, depression, PMT, stretch marks, low stomach acid and birth defects. Classic signs of zinc deficiency are lack of sense of taste and smell, and white spots and patches on the fingernails. Dosage: 15–50mg a day (very high doses of zinc should be avoided as they will interfere with iron absorption). If in doubt, consult a nutritional therapist.

Magnesium (Mg)

Yet another mineral used by the endocrine system is magnesium. It is a necessary aid in the manufacture of DNA and essential to the nervous system. where it acts as a natural tranquilliser. It restores adrenal function, as every time we make adrenaline we use magnesium. It is depleted by stress, alcohol, laxatives and diuretics. Classic signs of deficiency are tremors and cramps. It is best taken in the form of magnesium ascorbate. Dosage: 1000–3000mg a day (maintenance dose).

Calcium (Ca)

This is a mineral well supplied in most people's diets, although not well utilised on its own without magnesium. It is most commonly taken in supplements as calcium carbonate (chalk) or calcium phosphate, but this does not resemble any of the calciums that the body recognises as a nutrient. When we need calcium it is more sensible to eat vegetables grown in calcium-rich soil. Vegetables use calcium for stalks and other supportive parts, changing it into a form that we can absorb and utilise. If you really hate eating green vegetables and need extra calcium, take it as calcium citrate in a formula containing magnesium (Citrase from Biocare).

Chromium (Cr)

Not well absorbed from the diet, chromium is available in tiny amounts in whole foods such as grains. There is none whatsoever in refined foods. Within our body it can be found concentrated in small amounts in the adrenal glands, skin, fat, brain and muscle. Along with nicotinicacid (B3) and amino acids it makes up what is called the Glucose Tolerance Factor (GTF), improving insulin's effectiveness as a sugar regulator to pick up and store circulating sugar. It prevents late onset diabetes and hypoglycemia and treats high cholesterol levels. It is best taken as chromium polynicotinate drops (from Biocare) or chromium piccolinate (from Solgar).

Antioxidants

Vitamins A, C and E and the mineral trace element selenium, along with betacarotene, act together to prevent fats in the body becoming rancid or oxidised and thus help to prevent cancer (see p. 52 for further details on antioxidants). Brown patches and spots on the hands and arms are a sign of antioxidant deficiency. This isn't only happening on the outside, which is the part of us we see – it's also happening to your brain. There are many antioxidant supplements on the market, including products from Biocare, Solgar and Quest.

Recommended Supplement Regime

- Multivitamin/mineral capsule: one daily.
- Antioxidant: one daily.
- Vitamin C (as magnesium ascorbate): 1–3g daily. For acute infections and more serious problems take up to 10g daily.

If you are unsure about supplementation or are suffering from a serious or long-standing disease, consult a properly trained nutritionist. (See Useful Addresses.)

Illustrated Techniques of Application

Resting Massage

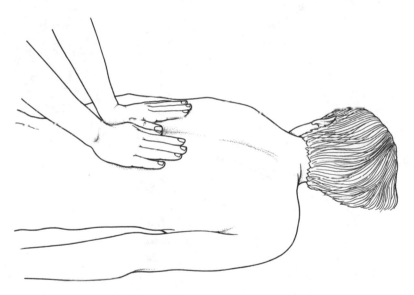

Resting Massage 1

Have your partner lie down with a pillow under the tummy or chest so that the body is comfortable. Oil your hands, place them on the lower back and, with even pressure, glide up towards the shoulders. Slide your hands out across the shoulders and gently return to the lower back. Repeat this gentle, rhythmic movement for ten minutes or so. Use very light pressure for someone who is highly emotional and firmer pressure for someone who is tired, depressed or recovering from illness. This technique requires the use of oil.

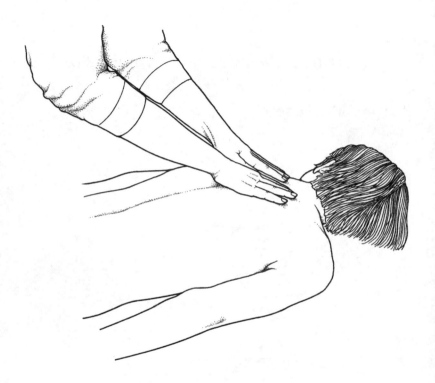

Resting Massage 2

Using your fingertips (the pads of your fingers, not the nails), rotate and press the flesh on either side of the spine, just below the base of the neck. This area stores tension and can become hard to the touch. Gentle yet firm massage given regularly is far better than a one-off strong massage which may be extremely painful. This technique can be used without oil but is more effective when oil is used.

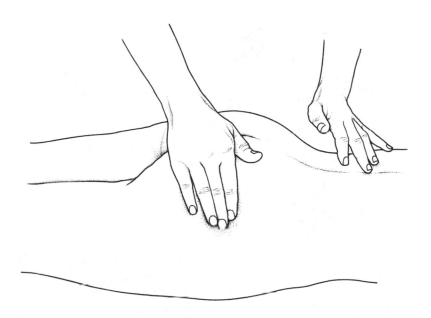

Resting Massage 3

Massaging the sides of the buttocks is a very useful, quick way of relieving tension in this part of the body, and can relieve constipation. Use the fingers of one hand to press and rotate the flesh in a circular motion. Oil needs to be used for this technique.

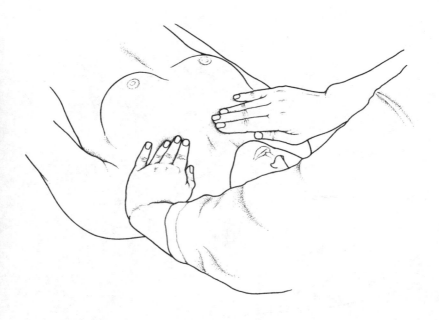

Resting Massage 4

Have your partner lie on their back and apply a little oil to your fingers. Place your hands on the chest just below the collar bone, with the fingertips of each hand meeting over the breastbone. Apply firm, even pressure to this area as you slide your hands across to the shoulders. This technique can be used after any type of neck, head or back massage, as it helps the lymphatic system to drain away the toxins released from the tissues.

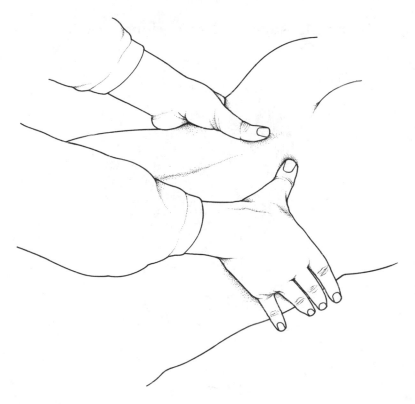

Resting Massage 5

Your partner should be lying on their tummy, with a small pillow to support them under the chest or tummy. Apply a little oil to your fingertips and place your hands on your partner's waist, positioning yourself to one side and facing their feet. Using firm pressure, rotate your thumbs in small circles, massaging the flesh at either side of the spine. Continue to press and rotate your thumbs whilst slowly moving away from the spine, until all the lower back area has been covered. Now reposition your hands a little further up the spine and repeat the movements.

Sitting Massage for Neck, Upper Back and Groin

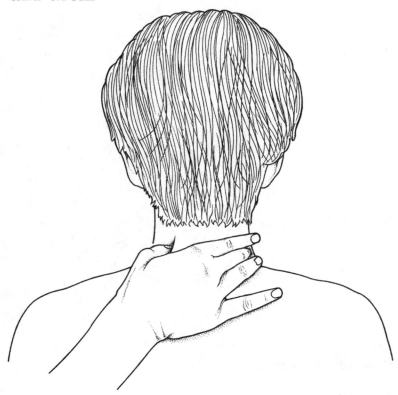

Sitting Massage 1

Place your thumb and second finger on either side of your partner's neck, level with the shoulders. Gently press and rotate the fingers, supporting your partner's head with your other hand if necessary. Slowly work your way up the neck. This technique may be used with or without essential oils.

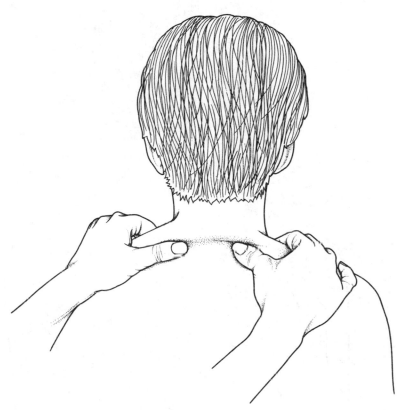

Sitting Massage 2

Place your hands on your partner's shoulders, with your thumbs towards the top of the spine. With gentle, firm pressure, push the flesh towards your fingers and hold. Repeat this movement, moving the thumbs slightly apart, so that all of the shoulder area is eventually covered. This technique can be used with or without oil.

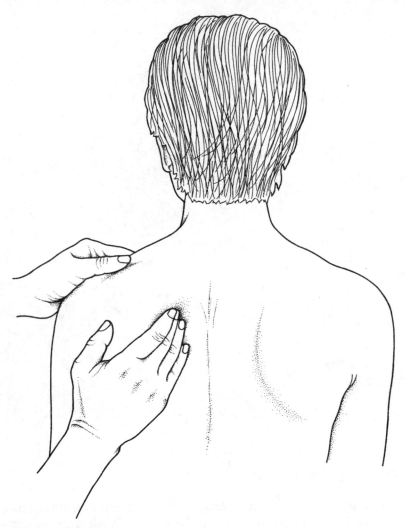

Sitting Massage 3

Support your partner's shoulder with one hand, then
slide the fingers into the fleshy area between the spine
and the shoulder blade. Massage the area of flesh from
mid-back up to the base of the neck. This technique works
best with oil.

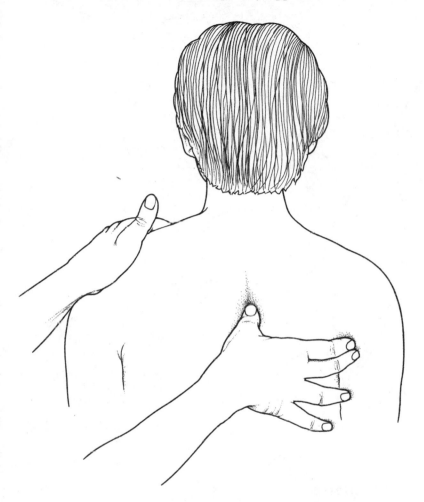

Sitting Massage 4

Hold your partner's shoulder with one hand. Use thumb
pressure with the other hand to locate any sore spot.
Press and rotate your thumb over the sore area. Press and
hold until the discomfort lessens. This technique may be
used with or without oil.

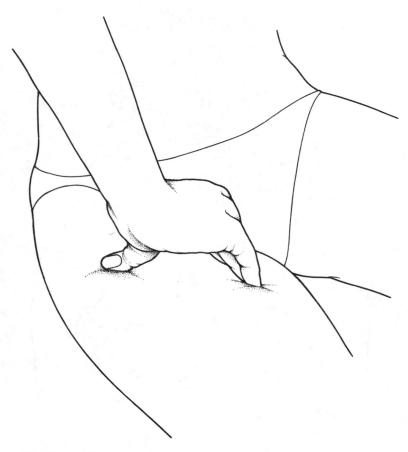

Sitting Massage 5

Either sit or kneel, depending on what is more comfortable, and locate the area of thigh close to the groin. This area is generally very tender (even ticklish) and lies directly over a large collection of lymph nodes. Use firm fingertip pressure to stimulate them.

Self-massage

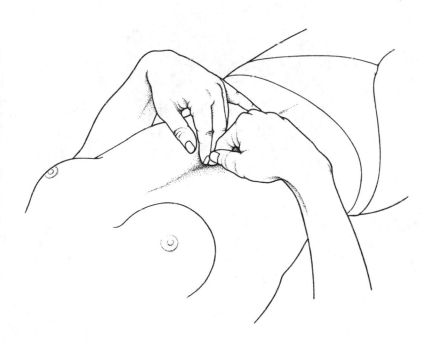

Self-massage 1

Solar plexus massage. This releases tension, whether from anger, overworking the brain, nervous tension or over-exertion. First locate the solar plexus, which is halfway between the navel and the bottom of the rib-cage. Take a deep breath and, as you exhale, press down with your fingertips and hold. Release the pressure and start again. This technique may be used with or without essential oils.

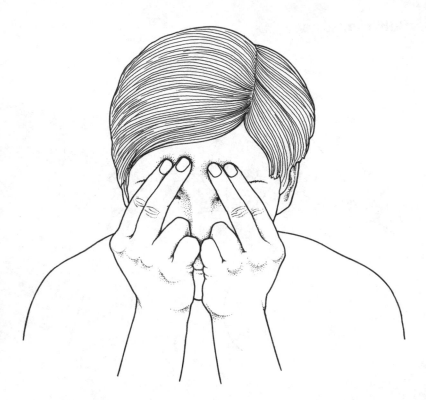

Self-massage 2

Forehead holding point. This technique releases mental
tension and can bring about an instant reduction in a 'hot
head'. Place first two fingers of each hand on the forehead
above the eyebrows, directly over the inner corner of the
eye. Hold very gently and you will feel a pulse. Continue
to hold whilst concentrating on the pulsation for at least
a minute or two.

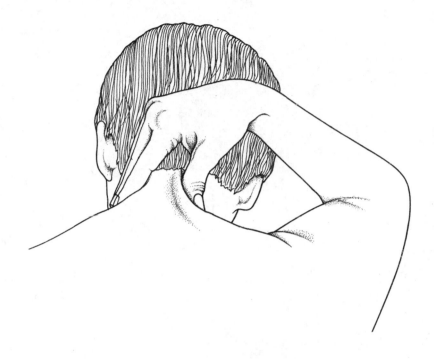

Self-massage 3

Neck massage. Lightly grip the back of your neck between your thumb and fingers, then rotate your moving
hand slowly from the base of the neck to the head. This
technique may be used with or without essential oils.

Self-massage 4

Scalp massage. Slide your fingers under your hair to the
scalp and, using moderate fingertip pressure, massage the
entire scalp area as though you are washing your hair.
This technique may be used without essential oils.

Compresses and Baths

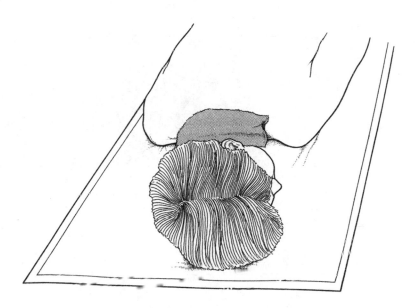

Compress 1

Neck compress made from face flannel. Dip a flannel into warm or cold aromatic water (use two or three drops of essential oil to 1 pint/½ litre of water). The temperature of the compress is a matter of personal preference and time of year. Warm or cold, it may be used to treat headaches, migraine and neck tension.

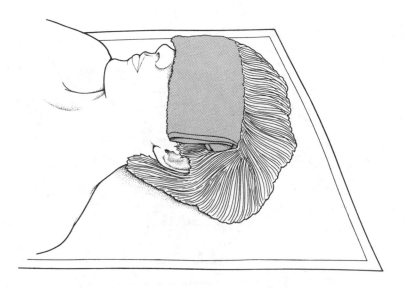

Compress 2

Forehead compress made from face flannel, large hand-kerchief or similar item. Use two or three drops of essential oil to 1 pint/½ litre of cold or luke-warm water). Use for the treatment of headaches, migraine, depression and other negative moods, insomnia and when you are feeling hot and bothered.

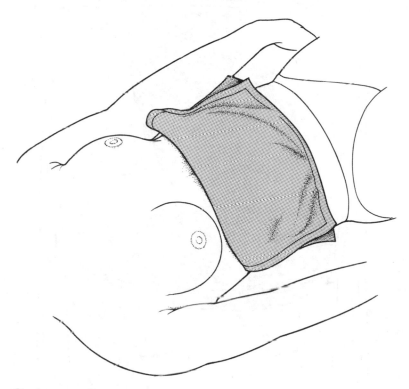

Compress 3

Tummy compress made from small hand towel. Use four or five drops of essential oil to 2 pints/1 litre water of comfortable temperature and mix well. Wring out compress, apply to tummy and cover with a dry towel. Use to treat nausea, indigestion and 'sick headaches'.

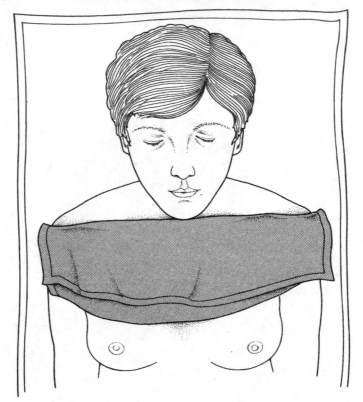

Compress 4

Chest compress made from a face flannel or a small hand
towel. Use four or five drops of essential oil to 2 pints/1
litre of water, which should be comfortably warm. Wring
out compress, apply to upper chest and cover with a dry
towel. Use to treat asthma, palpitations and panic attacks.

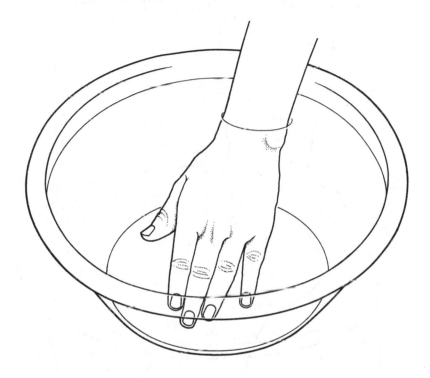

Hand Bath

Use water which is a comfortable temperature. Add five to six drops of essential oil to 1½ to 2 litres water and mix well. Place one hand in the water, palm down, and leave to soak for five to ten minutes or longer if preferred. Repeat with your other hand. If the bowl is large enough place both hands in together.

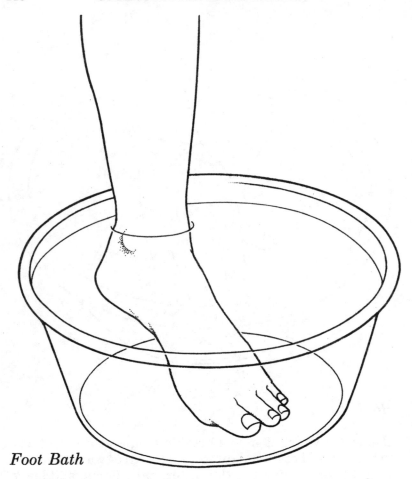

Foot Bath

As with the hand bath, mix 5–6 drops of essential oils into
a bowl of water (2 litres or so) before immersing feet. Soak
feet for as long as you feel comfortable.

Inhalation

To 1 pint/½ litre of hot (not boiling) water add three drops of essential oil. If you feel uncomfortable with hot steam inhalations, add a cup or two of cold water. Cover your head with a towel and breathe naturally.

Foot Massage

This massage technique is a wonderful way to de-stress your partner. However, it is important to wash your hands thoroughly afterwards as a lot of negative energy can flow from the foot to the hand.

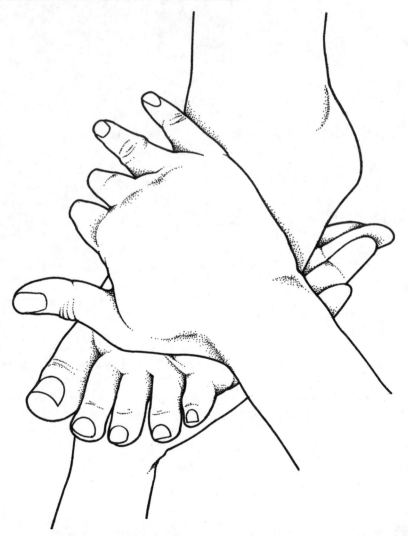

Foot Massage 1

Apply oil to your own hands before taking your partner's foot between your palms, holding the instep and heel. Slowly and firmly draw your hands towards you so that your palms meet as you slide over the toes. Repeat several times, slowly and with even pressure.

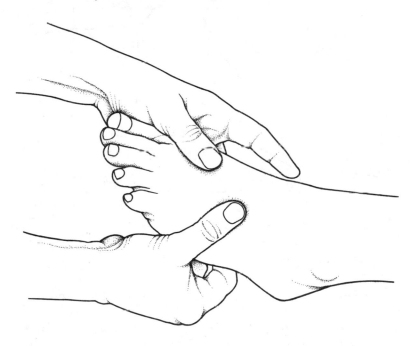

Foot Massage 2

Using your thumbs, apply gentle pressure to the area in between the bones of the foot, and glide from the toe webbing up to the arch. Repeat this process right across the top of the foot. Take the toe webbing between your thumb and forefinger, and squeeze gently.

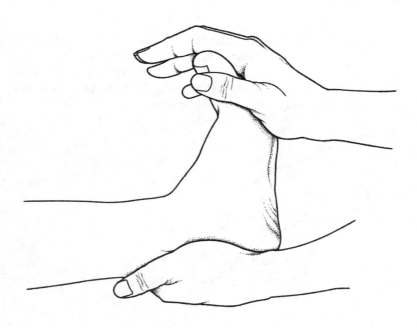

Foot Massage 3

Place one hand under your partner's ankle/heel and with your other hand gently push the foot away from you whilst gently drawing the heel towards you. Then take one toe at a time and gently rotate it.

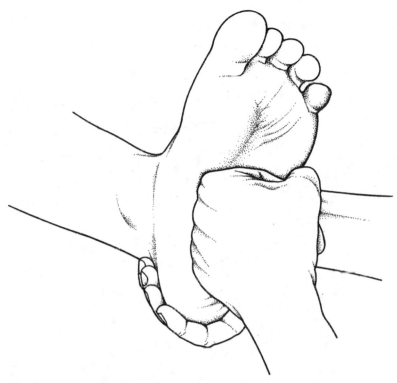

Foot Massage 4

Hold your partner's foot in one hand and form your other hand into a fist. Press the fist into the arch of the foot for a count of ten. Keeping skin contact, relax the pressure so that light contact is still being made between fist and the sole of the foot.

Hand Massage for Partner

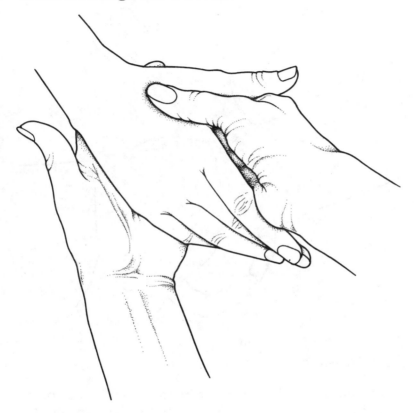

Hand Massage 1

Apply oil to your own palms before taking your partner's hand. Support the weight of your partner's arm by holding their hand (as shown), then glide the thumb of your other hand from the knuckle up to the wrist in the natural groove between the bones. Repeat until all the grooves have been treated.

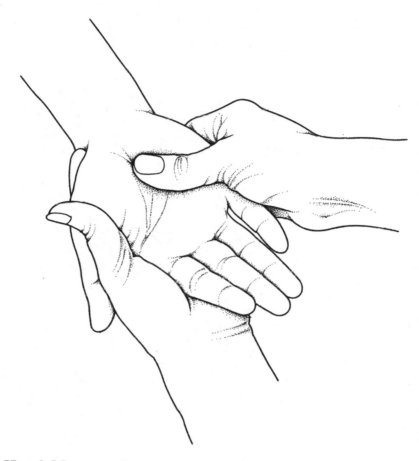

Hand Massage 2

Turn your partner's hand so that the palm is uppermost.
Use your thumbs to massage the entire palm, whilst
supporting the weight of your partner's hand. (If you
prefer, you can place a small towel across your knee
and rest your partner's hand on that.)

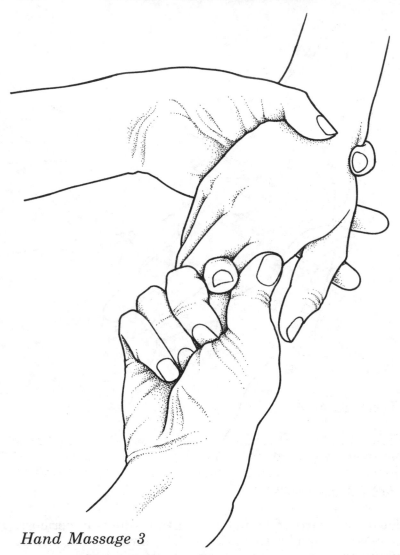

Hand Massage 3

Support your partner's hand with your left hand and with your right grip his or her finger close to the palm. Then slowly squeeze and pull the finger until you reach the fingertip. Apply slightly more pressure to the fingertip as you slide off. Treat each finger and thumb in this way.

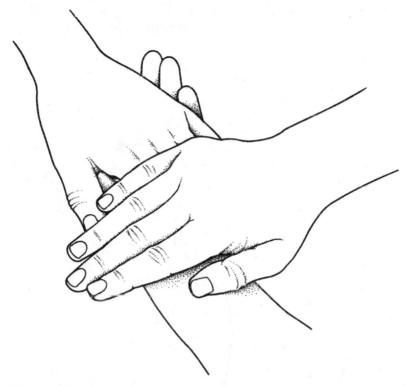

Hand Massage 4

Finish the hand massage by taking your partner's hand between your two palms and glide your hands down to the fingertips. Repeat several times, as this movement is very relaxing and comforting.

Hand Massage: Self-massage

This technique is very useful when you are stuck in traffic and the tension in your hands is extending to your arms, shoulders and neck (do it without oil in this case). It is also excellent for keyboard operators, and its regular use may help to prevent repetitive strain injury.

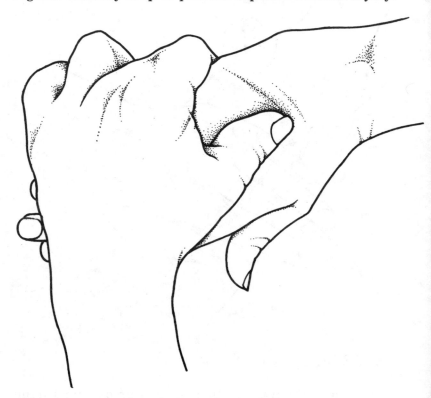

Hand Massage 5

Same as Hand Massage 1, but doing it to yourself.

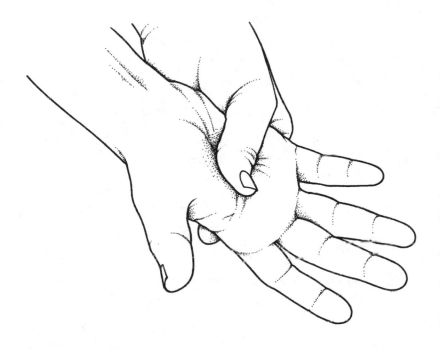

Hand Massage 6

Open out your hand as much as possible and, with the thumb of the other hand, press and massage the fleshy part of the palm from the wrist to the fingers. With forefinger and thumb, squeeze the webbing between fingers and gently massage it.

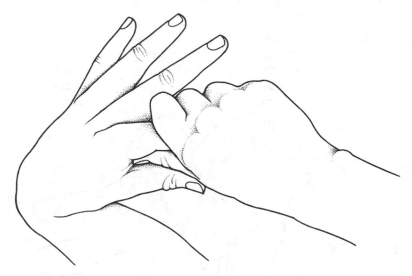

Hand Massage 7

Same as Hand Massage 3, but doing it to yourself.

Face Massage

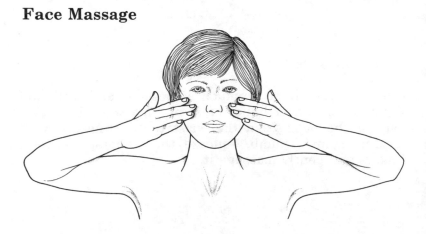

Face Massage 1

Gentle stroking movement of the cheeks is very soothing.
Apply oil to your fingers and, starting at the side of the
nose, sweep your hands across your cheeks, ending the
movement at the hairline. Then move the starting position a little further down the nose and repeat the sweep-
ing movement of the hands, ending at the ear. Continue
until all of the face has been covered.

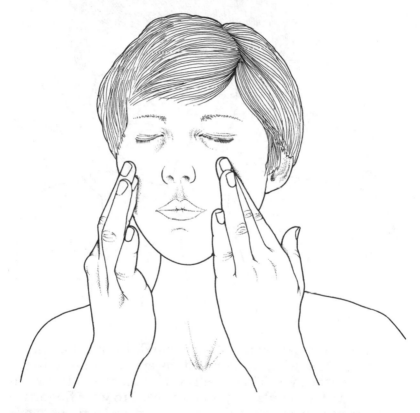

Face Massage 2

Locate the sinus points, by feeling for indentations in the
bones directly beneath the eye sockets, and level with the
centre of the eyes. With the second finger of each hand,

press this point and hold for a count of ten. This technique may be used with or without oil, and is easily incorporated into a face massage.

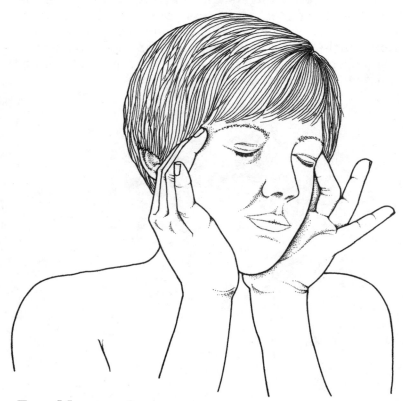

Face Massage 3

With the second finger of each hand, locate the temple points by following the curve of the eyebrows down to the corner of the eyes. This area is very delicate and you will be able to feel a pulse. Apply a little oil to your fingertips and gently massage this area, or merely touch your fingers to the pulse and hold for a few seconds. This technique can be used alone or incorporated into a face massage.

An A–Z of Stress-related conditions

So many of our twentieth century ailments have their origins in stress, and yet we often fail to recognise stress as the precipitating factor in our illness. This section of the book takes a look at many of today's most common stress-related ailments and gives advice on the aromatic way to help the condition, as well as giving general guidance. By no means conclusive, the A–Z section covers thirty-five stress-related conditions.

Abdominal pain (see Stomach ache)
Acne
Alopecia
Amenorrhea
Anxiety
Appetite, decreased or increased
Arthritis (see Joint pains)
Asthma
Back pain
Bad breath (see Halitosis)
Baldness (see Alopecia)
Blood pressure (see Hypertension)
Candida Albicans
Chronic Fatigue Syndrome (see Post Viral Syndrome)
Colds and flu
Cold sores (see Herpes)
Colic (see Indigestion)
Concentration lacking

Constipation
Cystititis
Depression
Diarrhoea
Dysmenorrhoea
Dyspepsia (see Indigestion)
Eczema
Fatigue
Fibrositis (see Shoulder pain)
Fungal infections (see Candida albicous)
Haemorrhoids (see Constipation)
Hair loss (see Alopecia)
Halitosis
Headaches and migraine
Heart attack (see Recovery from heart attack)
Heartburn (see Indigestion)
Herpes
Hypertension
Hyperventilation
IBS (Irritable Bowel Syndrome)
Immune deficiency
Impotence (see Sexual problems)
Indigestion
Insomnia
Irritability (see Tension)
Irritable Bowel Syndrome
Joint pains
Lethargy (see Fatigue)
Menstruation (absent) (see Amenorrhea)
Menstruation (painful) (see Dysmenorrhea)
Migraine (see Headache and migraine)
ME (Myalgic encephalitis) (see Post Viral Syndrome)
Nausea and vomiting
Neck pain
Nosebleed
Overeating (see Appetite decreased or increased)
Pain (see Back pain, joint pain, neck pain, shoulder pain)
Post Viral Syndrome
Psoriasis

Recovery from heart attack
Restlessness (see Tension)
Rheumatoid arthritis (see Joint pain)
Sexual problems
Shingles
Shoulder pain
Sleep problems (see Insomnia)
Stomach ache
Tension
Thrush (see Candida)
Viral infections (see Colds and flu, Immune deficiency, Post Viral Syndrome)
Vomiting (see Nausea and vomiting)

An A–Z of Stress-related Conditions

Acne

This common but unpleasant and unsightly inflammatory disease afflicts most of us at some time during our life. The condition is caused by a complex interaction in which an increase in production of the hormone androgen leads to an increase in the size and activity of the sebaceous glands in the skin. This in turn produces an oversecretion of the oily substance called sebum that lubricates the skin. The surplus sebum blocks and clogs the pores, creating a perfect breeding ground for bacterial infection.

Acne usually begins at puberty when the hormones are is in upheaval, but may develop at any time of hormonal disruption, including those precipitated by stress. Medical management involves the use of topical preparations such as retinoic acid, which is highly irritating to already sensitive skin, or, for more severe acne, a long-term course of antibiotics. The latter approach tends to lower overall vitality and its most common side-effect, vaginal THRUSH, is as unpleasant for women as the original condition. If these methods fail, oral contraceptives are advocated for at least six months in an attempt to balance the hormonal system.

General Guidelines

As with all stress-related conditions, the whole person and not just the specific condition should be taken into account. A sensible diet, high in nutrients and vitamins and low in fats, refined sugar, additives and preservatives, is crucial, as is drinking plenty of water. Stimulants such as nicotine, alcohol, coffee, tea and even chocolate are best avoided. A daily routine of exercise and fresh air not only builds morale and lessens stress, but helps improve circulation and increase lymphatic drainage.

Aromatic Solutions

Just as acne is caused by many factors interacting to produce disorder, its treatment too has many aspects. These include cleansing the skin; combating bacteria; regulating hormone balance and sebum secretion; detoxifying the system; and, finally, encouraging the regeneration of healthy new skin tissue.

In addition to the general guidelines on confronting and coping with stress presented in Chapter 5, I strongly recommend morning and evening baths with an essential oil blend. This not only helps soothe an over-wrought nervous system but also encourages the detoxification of impurities and the healthy regrowth of tissue.

Morning Bath Oil Blends
5–6 drops bergamot *or* 2 drops geranium *or* 3 drops juniper *or* 4 drops lemon

Night-time Bath Oil Blends
4 drops lavender *or* 4 drops myrtle *or* 4 drops orange *or* 3 drops ylang-ylang

Each of these aromatic bath blends is lovely in its own right, and the choice can be left to your personal preference.

To accelerate the detoxifying effect of the essential oils I recommend daily skin brushing as part of your aromatic bathing ritual. After soaking for ten minutes or so, take a medium-bristle nailbrush and gently stroke it down the sides and back of your neck, from the hairline down to the shoulders. Then, using firmer strokes, sweep the bristles over and under the collar bone, from the sternum (breastbone) across the chest to the armpit. This simple technique will help your lymphatic system to take away all the unwanted debris from the face and neck area, and assist in eliminating it from your body.

Aromatic Solutions

Since the underlying problem is stress, all the essential oils recommended in the following acne blends are also soothing and calming to the nervous system.

Oils for Acne

Oils	Cleansing	Antibacterial	Balancing	Detoxifying	Regenerating
Bergamot	*	*	*		
Camomile	*	*			
Cypress	*			*	
Geranium	*		*	*	
Juniper	*	*		*	
Lavender		*			▲
Neroli		*			*
Palmarosa		*	*		*
Ravansara		*			
Sandalwood	*	*			
Thyme-linalol	*	*		*	
Verbena		*			*

Cleansing
It is most important to remove surface dirt and dead tissue and to prepare the skin properly for essential oils. Cleansing should be done regularly every morning and every evening before going to bed. Please avoid the temptation, however great, to touch, squeeze or pick at your skin, as this only leads to infection of other areas and possible scarring.

Skin Cleanser for Acne

100ml bottled water
1 teaspoon cider vinegar
7 drops bergamot *or*
3 drops geranium *or*
3 drops lavender *or*
7 drops palmarosa

Massage
When it comes to the use of essential oils on acne-infected skin, the choice becomes a very personal one. Some people like to massage their face at night with a blend of essential oils such as the one listed below, while others loathe the feeling of a fatty oil on their skin and will only use face masks and cleansing lotions. A third option is to facial-steam your skin two or three times a week, while also maintaining a thorough daily cleansing routine. The choice has to be yours, but whichever option suits you, the outcome should prove to be the same: the combination of anti-bacterial/anti-inflammatory essential oils will penetrate deep into the dermis, the lower layer of skin to counteract inflammation, destroy bacteria and lessen the severity of your acne.

Night-time Acne Blend
10 ml base oil 5m/s (5m/s jojoba/5m/s sweet almond oil) 1 drop bergamot 1 drop lavender 2 drops orange

For a 100ml bottle of oil, simply multiply all the ingredients by ten.

Maintenance
This daily routine of bathing, facial cleansing and evening massage is best continued for as long as the acne and/or stress persists. Once the acute eruptions have subsided, in addition to twice-daily cleansing a simple and inexpensive facial mask can be used two or three times a week for a week or so, and then twice-weekly, as part of your maintenance programme.

Facial Mask for Acne
2 tablespoons fuller's earth powder or green clay ½ teaspoon runny honey 2 drops myrtle *or* bergamot *or* lavender *or* palmarosa Sufficient water to mix into a smooth yet thick consistency

Spread this mixture evenly over the face, forehead and chin, avoiding the eyes and lips. Leave on for between five and fifteen minutes, then rinse off with cold or lukewarm water and finish by splashing your face with clean cold water.

A flawless complexion is not gained overnight, and your commitment and persistence are vital to success. However, given time, improvement in the appearance and texture of your skin will reflect an overall improvement in you.

Other Alternatives
Homeopathy, reflexology, shiatsu, vitamin therapy.

Alopecia

We all consider thick, shining hair a sign of health and vitality; conversely, problems with hair usually signal underlying physiological disorders or severe mental strain. Hair thinning or hair loss may result from genetic factors, hormonal changes such as pregnancy or menopause, local disease such as PSORIASIS, severe diseases with high fevers, thyroid or pituitary deficiency or even overdoses of vitamin A. These and other conditions need to be ruled out by your doctor, but even if you are suffering from one of these, an aromatherapy treatment programme may be helpful to reduce hair loss and encourage regrowth.

Alopecia areata is a medical term for sudden hair loss in well-defined patchy areas, without any obvious medical explanation. Unlike true baldness, which is a natural but permanent process, alopecia areata can develop in men or women of any age and is usually a temporary condition with a good prognosis. These days more and more cases of alopecia areata in women are being seen by doctors, as businesswomen become high fliers and take on stresses and responsibilities in what was once a male domain.

Any hairy area may be involved, although the scalp and beard are the most common sites. Patches are not inflamed and may be single or multiple, and generally about the size of a 50 pence coin. The cause of alopecia areata is somewhat mysterious, although stress is now considered a primary factor. Following shock, grief or prolonged stress and strain, the immune system begins to self-destruct, which in this case is manifested by interruption of the normal cycle of hair growth.

General Guidelines

If you are undergoing stress significant enough to produce alopecia areata, the last thing you want is a patchy scalp and the embarrassment that it may cause. Now is the time to be gentle with yourself – and with your hair. Pamper yourself with lovely fragrant baths to lift your spirits and consider treating yourself to a professional aromatherapy massage.

Morning Stress-reducing Bath Blends

2 drops clary sage
2 drops lemon
2 drops palmarosa
2 drops rosemary

Night-time Stress-reducing Bath Blends

4 drops lavender
4 drops verbena

Or choose any two oils from the following list, adding three to four drops of each to a full bath.

Morning	Evening
Cypress	Clary sage
Geranium	Geranium
Lemon	Lavender
Melissa	Rose
Palmarosa	Verbena
Rosemary	Ylang-ylang
Thyme-linalol	

Avoid hair dyes and chemical-based shampoos and conditioners, and try to limit washing your hair to once or twice weekly. Protect your scalp from chlorinated swimming pools, polluted bathing areas and any other unnecessary toxins. And, as always, eat sensibly: a healthy diet rich in protein and vegetable fats, with regular vitamin B and C supplements, goes a long way to help regain a healthy head of hair.

Aromatic Solutions

Several essential oils, including lavender, rosemary and thyme, increase the circulation to the head and stimulate the hair follicles to grow. Among the base oils, jojoba is a traditional remedy for hair growth among the native people of Mexico and Arizona and a favourite of mine for aromatic hair care blends; so is olive oil, which has been used to thicken hair since antiquity.

If you have a well-defined bald patch on your scalp, I recommend a night-time treatment lotion to be used every night for four to six weeks. Apply the blend all over your scalp, gently massage it into your skin for ten to fifteen minutes and then leave it in your hair. Also massage the lotion into the sides and back of your neck. This not only releases muscle tension but stimulates the cervical lymph nodes to drain away toxins and waste matter from the scalp. Good sleep is an important facet of stress reduction, and this blend of essential oils will promote restful sleep while encouraging the regrowth of strong healthy hair.

Night-time Treatment Lotion for Alopecia
100ml bottled water 1 teaspoon cider vinegar 15 drops clary sage 3 drops geranium 20 drops lavender 5 drops verbena

Shake very thoroughly and pour a little into the palm of one hand. Apply to the scalp and neck as you would a cologne or aftershave to the face, then, using fingertip massage, gently work the lotion into your scalp as though you were washing your hair.

Once or twice weekly, before shampooing with the shampoo below, apply alopecia hair conditioner to the affected area. Massage the blend into your scalp, wrap your head in hot towels to increase absorption of oils and leave on for at least thirty minutes. Then wash off.

Hair Shampoo for Alopecia
200 ml unperfumed shampoo 5 drops lemon 5 drops palmarosa 5 drops rosemary 5 drops thyme-linalol

Tilt bottle to mix before use.

Alopecia Hair Conditioner
100ml jojoba 20 drops cypress 20 drops lavender 20 drops lemon 20 drops palmarosa 20 drops rosemary 20 drops thyme-linalol

Other Alternatives

Homeopathy, hypnotherapy, psychotherapy, vitamin therapy.

Amenorrhoea

Absence of menstruation may be caused by any disease that disturbs the function of the ovaries, either by an inability to produce the necessary hormones or by dysfunction in the hormone-regulating system which is controlled by the hypothalamus and the pituitary gland. So while the list of possible causes of amenorrhoea is very long indeed, one of the more common precipitators is stress. Researchers do not yet understand precisely how psychic stimuli, such as anxiety, can result in the cessation of monthly periods, but clearly it is one of nature's most intelligent ways of sparing an anxious or overwrought woman the burdens of pregnancy.

If you are convinced that the cessation of your periods is not the result of a systemic or local disease, a congenital or physical abnormality, or an after-effect of chemical therapy such as withdrawal from oral contraceptives, console yourself that in time your body will right itself – once the underlying stress has lifted.

General Guidelines

Believing in your body's ability to heal itself may sound like foolish advice, but the powers of nature to create equilibrium are more sure than any man-made treatment. In addition, resting calm in the knowledge that your hormonal system will return to normal helps reduce your overall stress level.

A nutritious diet is very important and in extreme cases, such as anorexia or obesity, poor diet can actually cause the problem. (If you know that your lack of periods is due to weight reduction as well as stress, see APPETITE, DECREASED OR INCREASED).

Aromatic Solutions

Essential oils can help speed things along by working on two fronts: to soothe, relax and ease your distress; and to encourage your hormonal cycle towards balance. Start experimenting with calming oils in an aromatic burner or as perfume. Combinations of a few drops of geranium and rose, or of clary sage and melissa, add a quiet aura to the environment when burnt in a vaporizer or worn on the body. Select from the following list according to your smell preference, budget and availability.

Oils to Stimulate Menstruation
Camomile Marjoram Melissa Myrrh Rose Lavender Geranium Cypress Clary Sage Thyme-linalol

Massage
Nature has provided us with a handful of essential oils which have hormone-like properties, and these can be useful in reinstating regular menstrual periods and restoring fertility. Choose one, two or three essences from the above list and, using a total of 7 drops essential oil to 2 teaspoons fatty base oil such as sweet almond oil, massage your abdomen and lower back each day for several weeks (see p. 99 for technique).

The following blend is recommended, but is, of course, only one example. The fragrance as well as the action of the essential oils is important, and you should choose those essences which appeal to you most.

Massage Blend for Amenorrhoea
15 ml sweet almond 2 drops angelica 3 drops clary sage 2 drops geranium

Be sure to set aside a quiet time of the day or evening for your massage. Put on some relaxing music and turn up the heat if necessary, so that the room is at a comfortable temperature. Use these moments to relax fully while you visualise your ovaries becoming healthy and strong.

Other Alternatives

Acupuncture, applied kiniesiology, cranio-sacral therapy, homeopathy, hypnotherapy, reflexology, shiatsu, vitamin therapy.

Anxiety

Different from fear in that it has no object, anxiety therefore cannot lessen when the danger has passed. In fear the primitive responses to fight or flee may provide a resolution, but with anxiety the release of adrenalin has no outlet in action. Instead it tends to accumulate, increasing the sense of unease. While most of us attempt to attach our anxiety to a specific situation, in the end we often find that the state is elusive and subjective, reflecting our deepest fears and concerns rather than objective reality.

Stress obviously comes to us in various forms and levels of impact, but when too prolonged or too severe it will inevitably set off our own personal time-bomb of anxiety. Any discussion of coping with stress must of necessity consider one of its most common consequences: anxiety.

Anxiety breeds a multitude of problems such as restlessness, TENSION, irritability, inability to concentrate (see CONCENTRATION LACKING), panic attacks, STOMACH ACHE, loss of appetite (see APPETITE, DEPRESSED OR

INCREASED), butterflies in the stomach, HYPERVENTILA-
TION, chest pain, dry mouth, faintness/dizziness, HEAD-
ACHES, reduced sexual drive (see SEXUAL PROBLEMS),
palpitations, NAUSEA, INSOMNIA, excessive sweating and
DIARRHOEA.

Essential oils are one of nature's best tools for lessening anxiety, and the list of helpful ones is extensive.

Essential Oils to Lessen Anxiety
Angelica
Bergamot
Camomile
Clary sage
Cypress
Frankincense
Geranium
Juniper
Lavender
Marjoram
Melissa
Neroli
Rose
Rosewood
Sandalwood
Verbena
Vetivert
Ylang-ylang

General Guidelines

While you may not uncover the true cause of your
anxiety without help, I and like-minded people attribute
much of the anxiety in our modern world to a separation
from the source, an absence of faith, a nameless, bottom-
less sense of 'aloneness'. For all of us there may be times
when we feel an emptiness inside, on which anxiety

feeds. Remember, anxiety is just a feeling, your feeling. You own it. Acknowledge it, and let it go. In her book *Heart Thoughts* Louise Hay advises: 'Anxiety is fear and not trusting yourself. Just recognise it as the part that is used to us being upset about something and thank it for sharing and let it go.'

Most experts on anxiety would also recommend what I term 'cobweb-breaking' activities. For example, you could go out into the fresh air, work hard physically in a garden or an aerobic class, or see a friend and focus on her needs rather than yours. There are many helpful books on the subject. But try to avoid the escape routes of alcohol or drugs as they lead to a very dead end. I would also keep away from all stimulants – coffee, tea, cola drinks – and substitute herbal teas (camomile, lemon verbena and so on) or even warm milk.

Aromatic Solutions

Heaven and hell really do exist inside all of us. Hell for me is to be ensconced in a prolonged period of anxiety, unable to experience joy, peace or lightness of being. At these times it takes a conscious effort to rise above the inner turmoil and turn to the beautiful aromas of essential oils. Any of the oils listed on p. 149 can replace the anxious feelings with a sense of gratitude to the fragrant plant and to the power that put the fragrance in the plant.

One of the first steps you can take to lessen your anxiety is to breathe regularly and deeply. Resting comfortably while burning in a room fragrancer a few drops of sandalwood, frankincense or any of the listed oils will help you calm down and let your body relax, so that it may find its proper rhythm.

Just as each of us feels our anxiety uniquely, each of the essential oils has its own individual effects on mood and emotion. Brief descriptions of five common essential oils for lessening anxiety are given below, but any of the oils listed may be chosen and combined into bath oils, massage blends, perfumes or room fragrancers, or inhaled directly from their bottle in a moment of crisis. Enjoy the discovery of finding what works for you.

Geranium
This delightful oil with a sweet fresh floral scent helps to harmonise the emotions. Like bergamot and frankincense, it may have either a calming or an uplifting effect on the emotions, depending on your needs. It is therefore very useful for anxiety states when you need to regain your equilibrium.

Lavender
This oil is said to guard against unbridled emotions, so it is an excellent choice when anxiety is accompanied by agitation or mood swings. Lavender induces a sense of peacefulness and integration and is one of the best oils to use in the bath before bedtime, as it helps promote restful sleep.

Marjoram
One of the most calming of the essential oils, Marjoram is known to have been used as a tranquilliser by women in Ancient Greece, who rubbed it on their heads. The oil forms a barrier to the onslaught of stimuli and allows the emotions time to rest. Marjoram is therefore especially useful to induce sleep or to soothe free-floating fears.

Neroli
Extracted from the intensely fragrant white blossoms of the orange tree, neroli is one of the foremost tranquillisers among the essential oils. It was used in Victorian England to treat 'the vapours' and is superb at subduing frantic emotions, such as anxiety with panic.

Vetivert
This oil is a deeply relaxing and calming scent that is highly beneficial for relieving extreme anxiety, nervous

tension and insomnia. Called 'the oil of tranquillity', vetivert is said to protect against injury through over-sensitivity and to strengthen an inner determination to live life according to one's highest ideals.

Massage
Particularly beneficial for anxiety states, massage has a soothing, calming effect that encourages the parasympathetic nervous system to restore harmony by slowing down the heart rate, removing tension and promoting restful sleep. There is a tremendous choice of essential oils for anti-anxiety massage blends, and the search for your ideal can add a little bit of heaven to your life.

Anti-Anxiety Masssage Blend
10ml sweet almond 1 drop angelica 3 drops bergamot *or* petitgrain 2 drops rose *or* geranium

If it is not possible for you to be massaged by a friend or partner, or to visit an aromatherapist, you can help to relieve a tremendous amount of nervous tension simply by massaging your solar plexus (see p. 109 for technique).

Other Alternatives

Bach flower remedies, cranio-sacral therapy, homeopathy, hypnotherapy, NLP, reflexology.

Appetite, Decreased or Increased

In times of stress, the appetite is often affected. Like so many other functions, appetite is regulated by the hypothalamus, which in turn is linked to the emotional centres of the brain. Thus emotions, both positive (like being in love) and negative (like anger, sadness or grief) can cause some of us to stop eating, and others of us to over-eat. Extreme forms of these common patterns such as anorexia nervosa, bulimia or compulsive eating leading to obesity are beyond the scope of this book, although treatment from a professional therapist is often very helpful. For the rest of us with common-or-garden eating problems, using the essential oils in creative ways can help alleviate underlying anxiety and depression, as well as stimulate the desire for food or decrease the need for it, as the case may be.

General Guidelines

Whichever end of the eating spectrum you fall into exercise is one of the best overall aids. If you have trouble making yourself eat, exercise – especially if pleasurable – tends to reduce tension and release stress-relieving endorphins that generate a sense of calm and wellbeing. If you have trouble with over-eating, exercise similarly helps you feel good about yourself while burning up the calories.

When your appetite is low, it's important to prepare foods that your body craves, and not those you feel you *must* eat to stay healthy. Reductions in normal appetite are generally temporary and if for the short term you want only mashed potatoes, indulge yourself. Little and often is probably the healthiest way to eat, so feel free to snack, but avoid junk foods as they have no nutritional value.

If your appetite is increased, perhaps it would be wise to consider what the food is doing for you. Does eating give you comfort? Does it distract you from your worries? Does it pick you up or calm you down? By examining these issues you may discover why you are eating, and in so doing start a more positive, more fulfilling approach to achieving satisfaction.

Aromatic Solutions

Appetite decreased
The smell of food stimulates the appetite, as do certain essential oils such as rose. The Romans used this oil extensively during their banquets, and it is said that the wings of birds were sprinkled with rose oil to perfume the air at mealtimes. Although a less exotic alternative, burning essential oils in a room fragrancer is often recommended as a subtle enticement to eat. Oils to stimulate the appetite can be massaged gently over the abdomen and upper chest (see p. 99) an hour or so before eating.

Oils to Stimulate the Appetite
Angelica Bergamot Caraway Coriander Fennel Lemon Peppermint Rose

Aromatic 'Aperitif Massage'
10 ml sweet almond 2 drops coriander 2 drops lemon

Appetite increased
If there is true hunger and physical need, essential oils cannot be suppressive. If, however, the real need is for comfort or calm, the oils may be deeply nourishing (without the calories). Any of the aromatic bath blends

discussed in Chapter 5 will help you settle down and feel a sense of pleasure that is not related to eating.

If you are feeling unhappy about your body, now is the time to start a programme of aromatic body conditioning. A two-week aromatic slimming and toning regimen will help transform a negative impulse to eat into a more positive impulse to look and feel good. My book *The 14 Day Aromabeauty Plan* contains many suggestions for improving your 'problem areas', whether they are flabby thighs, sagging buttocks or any other part of your body.

Toning and Slimming Massage Blends
10 ml sweet almond 3 drops grapefruit 3 drops juniper *or* 2 drops lemon 1 drop lemongrass 3 drops orange

No toning or slimming programme is complete without proper detoxification. One of the best ways of detoxifying your body is to take daily aromatic baths and brush your skin while relaxing in the aromatic water. As the lymphatic system starts to function properly, toxins are removed, fat cells digested and proper metabolism reinstated, ensuring that your body takes what it needs from the food you eat, and eliminates what it doesn't need.

Other Alternatives

Acupuncture, homeopathy, hypnotherapy, NLP, psychotherapy, reflexology and vitamin therapy.

Asthma

Bronchial asthma is defined as reversible narrowing of
the air passages of the lungs due to varying spasm,
swelling of the mucous membranes, and excessive secretion of thick sticky mucus. Breathing in takes place in the
normal way, but only partial breathing out occurs, and
sufferers may experience severe wheezing and breathlessness. Attacks often occur at night and last one or
two hours.

There are two types of asthma: extrinsic and intrinsic.
Extrinsic asthma is common in children, especially boys,
who have inherited hypersensitivity to allergens such as
pollen, moulds, house dust and animal dander (skin cells
on hairs shed by pets). Attacks of extrinsic asthma tend to
become less frequent and less severe with age. Among
adult asthmatics, only 10–20 per cent have extrinsic
asthma while the majority have intrinsic asthma. In
the latter case, symptoms are triggered by non-allergic
factors such as respiratory infection, irritants like cigar-
ette smoke, or emotional states, particularly anxiety.

It is now known that stress can affect the immune
system and precipitate breakdowns in its functioning,
leading to the typical allergic response of asthma with
inflammation (see Chapter 2). Both extrinsic and intrinsic asthma may therefore be stress-related in susceptible
individuals, and furthermore may influence the severity
and progression of the disease. It is hardly surprising that
in these stressful times, one in seven people suffers from
asthma and requires medical care at some time.

Conventional drug therapy is aimed at dilating the
bronchial airways and reducing swelling and inflammation. Since all anti-asthma drugs have side-effects, some
of which are very serious and undesirable, I advocate
keeping these medicines at hand for emergency use, but
whenever possible avoiding them and following alternative approaches such as aromatherapy and homeopathy.
Asthma is a serious condition that may be life-threaten-

ing, and the choice of treatment must be made by you alone after exploration of the various options. Fortunately, even if you decide to follow other approaches aromatherapy may be highly effective – and safe – when used in acute conditions, and certainly when used in the prevention of asthma.

General Guidelines

If you suffer from asthma or have a child who does, you have probably already received advice on how to rid the home of allergens: daily thorough vacuuming and dusting; replacement of old mite-infested pillows; purchasing dehumidifiers to discourage mould and so on. This is important, but often impossible to accomplish entirely. Here, as in so many other situations, an ounce of prevention using the essential oils is worth a pound of cure using prescribed drugs.

Two of the most common triggers of asthma in susceptible people can be controlled automatically: first, reduction of anxiety before an attack occurs; and second, prevention of respiratory infections that frequently precede an attack. Techniques for lessening anxiety (see p. 148) can be followed when you feel yourself coming under attack.

In winter, during cold and flu epidemics or in congested office environments, vaporise air-purifying essences such as bergamot and thyme or spike lavender and ravansara to help prevent the spread of infection. If your resistance is low, also take morning and evening baths containing four drops of myrtle, four drops of lavender and one drop of either ravansara or tea tree.

Aromatic Solutions

At least once daily you can massage into your chest a relaxing blend of one teaspoon sweet almond oil containing four drops of *frankincense* and one drop of *angelica*. At the same time visualise your lungs expanding, your chest widening and clear, pure nourishing air entering your body. Then with each deep inward breath imagine a gate opening to let in light and joy, and with each outward breath the gate closing behind tension and fear.

During an acute attack, place two to three drops of anti-spasmodic essential oil into some warm water – over a candle fragrancer or even in a mug of hot water – and inhale it. Moisture helps to loosen mucus, and a few drops of lavender or clary sage in a humidifier will help stop spasms and keep you calm. If possible, add two drops of frankincense as well, since it both slows down and deepens the breathing, while inducing a sense of profound relaxation.

Anti-Spasmodic Essential Oils
Angelica Bergamot Camomile Clary sage Eucalyptus Frankincense Lavender Lemon Marjoram Melissa Neroli Niaouli Rose Thyme-linalol Verbena

Between attacks, have a friend or your partner massage your entire back and chest using light, rhythmic strokes (see pages 99–102 for techniques).

Asthma Blend for Bath or Massage
1 drop angelica 4 drops frankincense 3 drops lavender   *or* 3 drops bergamot 2 drops lemon 2 drops melissa

The same essences can be added to a full bath of warm water, or for a massage they may be added to 15ml sweet almond oil.

Other Alternatives

Asthma, cranio-sacral therapy, homeopathy, hypnotherapy, NLP, vitamin therapy.

Back Pain

Sometimes back pain is due to a specific and often serious physical disorder such as a slipped disc, a degenerative condition of the spine, kidney infection or gynaecological abnormality, and for this reason must always be checked out by your doctor. More often than not, however, back pain is the result of stress – either physical or mental. Bad posture, prolonged sitting or standing, even flat feet can force the muscles protecting the spine into awkward compensatory positions. These same muscles also respond to your stress and tension by tensing themselves. They do not respond independently of your emotions, but rather reflect them even if you are unaware of them or refuse to acknowledge them.

The other two common sites of stress-related muscle

tension are the neck (see NECK PAIN) and the shoulders (see SHOULDER PAIN).

General Guidelines

Since back pain is one of the most frequently encountered complaints in doctors' surgeries in the Western world, costing industry millions of pounds per year in sick pay and lost hours, there is no shortage of books and specialists to consult. Finding the right approach for you is often a matter of trial and error, but long-term relief requires a commitment to keeping your muscles supple and strong. If the muscles of both your back and stomach are no longer capable of supporting your torso, then strains and pains are inevitable. Advice on back stretches and stomach exercises can be had from numerous sources. Improving your posture, becoming strong through regular exercise and learning to unwind those tensed up muscles are not quick, magical solutions, but they are essential for a healthy back.

In an acute situation, when your back has given out and immobilised you, experts now recommend cold packs, rather than heat, to relieve the pain. A bag of frozen peas sitting on your back may look ridiculous, but works wonders! And remember to breathe deeply; a constricted muscle needs oxygen to function. The spasm will pass as you and your muscles begin to relax.

Aromatic Solutions

Essential oils, especially when combined with massage, can provide incredible relief for tense back muscles. The oils work in several ways: they encourage muscle expansion, increase blood flow and oxygen supply, and reduce any areas of pain and inflammation.

Oils for Back Pain
Black pepper Camomile Clary sage Cypress Eucalyptus Juniper Lavender Lemon Marjoram Myrtle Orange Peppermint Rosemary Thyme-linalol Vetivert

In a crisis, compresses of two drops of **rosemary**, two drops of lavender and two drops of marjoram in 1 litre of warm water can be applied directly to the affected area, or two drops of each of these essences can be added to a bath of comfortably warm water. If you can, book yourself a session with a professional aromatherapist; if this is not possible, enlist the help of a friend or your partner to give you an aromatic massage.

Massage Blend for Back Pain

10 ml sweet almond
1 drop black pepper
1 drop clary sage
2 drops lemon
1 drop orange
or   2 drops juniper
      3 drops lavender
      2 drops marjoram

Lie on your front and place a small pillow under your stomach to support your back. Make sure the room is pleasantly warm; any chilliness will cause your muscles to become tense, which will only create additional pain. Soft, soothing music in the background and several drops of myrtle or lavender in an aromatic burner add to the atmosphere of healing calm.

Other Alternatives

Acupuncture, homeopathy, McTimoney chiropractic, Cranio-sacral therapy, NLP, shiatsu.

Baldness

See ALOPECIA.

Blood Pressure

See HYPERTENSION.

Candida Albicans

Although candida albicans is a natural yeast that lives in a healthy body as a friendly organism, when the immune system is under-functioning the normal system of checks and balances breaks down, the yeast multiplies too rapidly and the effects are unpleasant. The most common causes of candidal infections are corticosteroids or antibiotic therapy, endocrine changes due to pregnancy, oral contraceptives, obesity, diabetes or prolonged stress. Usually the infection is limited to the skin and mucous membranes of the mouth and vagina, of which the organism is a normal occupant, but occasionally it may spread via the gastrointestinal tract. Given the widespread use of antibiotics, both in medication and in the meat that we eat the high consumption of sugar and the pervasive presence of stress in our culture, it is no surprise that candidal infection is one of the more common medical problems, along with its result – a weakened immune system.

Oral candidiasis appears as creamy white patches surrounded by a sore red area on the cheek, tongue and palate of the mouth. Vaginal candidiasis, popularly called thrush, causes a creamy white, irritating or itchy discharge from the vagina. Infection of the penis is less common, but may occur in the partner of an affected woman. Candidal paronychia or nailbed infection may begin after trauma, a hangnail or a rough manicure in which the skin is broken, or by chronic irritation, for example from excessive exposure to water and detergents.

The medical management of candida infections usually involves treatment with the antifungal nystatin, which generally only works in a palliative way. Although the problem may lessen over a period of weeks or months, the body is subjected to lengthy periods of drug therapy which further reduce the efficiency of the immune system.

General Guidelines

If a candidal infection has developed, the normal intestinal flora will need some help to fight off the organism. Eating plenty of live yogurt or taking yogurt tablets or lactobacillus capsules is often very effective. If you have had prolonged or repeated bouts of thrush, an anti-candida diet that drastically reduces the consumption of sugar, on which the organism thrives, may be provided by a nutritionist. In addition, because candida multiplies best in warm, moist environments, it is best to avoid putting your hands in water and to wear rubber gloves if your nails are affected; stay away from vaginal deodorants, bubblebath and tight-fitting, non-absorbent underwear if you have vaginal thrush. Cotton pants are recommended, as the natural fibre allows the skin to breathe. Sadly, you may infect your partner during sex, or reinfect yourself, unless 'protective' measures are taken.

Aromatic Solutions

Several essential oils are particularly helpful, not only for localised use but also on an emotional level – having vaginal thrush can make you feel very depressed. These oils can be used either in the bath, as a douche or in a sitz bath. Douche twice daily until relief has been obtained, and then two or three times a week until you are completely clear of symptoms. Alternatively you can place several drops of tea tree oil across the top and sides of a small tampon to make a vaginal pessary. Change the pessary at least twice in twenty-four hours, and use this treatment for a day or two to clear up minor infections.

Aromatic Douches for Candida Albicans
To 1 litre warm water add: 2 drops rose 4 drops lavender 2 drops bergamot *or* 6 drops tea tree

For more persistent vaginal or oral thrush, take three drops of niaouli and three drops of lemon oil with half a teaspoon of brown sugar. Many aromatherapists would argue that essential oils should never be taken internally, but in my experience this method is safe if limited to no more than two doses daily for a maximum of three weeks. Purity is essential, however, and you need to obtain those essential oils which are approved in France for medicinal purposes. If any stomach upset develops, either cut back the amount to one drop of niaouli and one drop of lemon, or cease taking them orally.

For oral thrush, make a mouthwash/gargle in the proportions of one drop niaouli and six drops lemon to 200ml water. Use several times a day until relief is obtained. Candida of the nailbed has a notoriously slow healing rate, and if you stop treatment too soon the symptoms quickly reappear. Apply a blend of six to ten drops of tea tree in one teaspoon jojoba oil until all signs of infection have vanished.

See IMMUNE DEFICIENCY and DEPRESSION for suggested daily bath recipes.

Other Alternatives

Applied kinesiology, homeopathy, vitamin therapy.

Chronic Fatigue Syndrome

See POST VIRAL SYNDROME.

Colds and Flu

There are at least a hundred different viruses that cause the common cold. All of them are easily spread through the air and all are resistant to modern medical treatment.

The symptoms of a cold are familiar to everyone: sneezy, stuffed up or runny nose, cough, scratchy throat and fatigue. With flu, add to these symptoms fever, general malaise, headache, aching sore muscles and tight chest. In addition, infected areas of the upper respiratory tract often fall prey to bacteria, and secondary bacterial infections of the ears, sinuses, throat or lungs are not uncommon.

Although cold viruses are very prevalent, they are only powerful when your body is run down and can no longer resist infection. Our susceptibility to colds and flu is more frequent in winter when our natural vitality is decreased, following prolonged fatigue or repeated infections, or because of stress. Colds may not be generally labelled as a stress-related condition, but you need only consider how often you or your family have become ill after a period of stress to recognise the connection. Stress lowers our immune system, making us vulnerable to all manner of internal and external factors, including viruses.

General Guidelines

There is some disagreement over whether vitamin therapy can prevent a cold, but high doses (5 grams) of vitamin C in the form of magnesium ascorbate certainly shorten its course. Obviously it is important to drink plenty of water or fruit juices, as liquids increase urination and the subsequent removal of toxins from the body. Bed rest may not be necessary, but taking it easy on yourself is: the long list of 'should dos' can wait a few days longer until you 'can do'.

I am against antibiotics on principle, but even the medical profession believes they should not be given for colds and flu as they have no effect on viral infections. If they are recommended by your doctor to prevent possible follow-on bacterial infection, perhaps you would like to consider aromatic preventive measures first. Antibiotics are like heavy artillery, and need not be called upon if essential oil therapy is working simply and effectively. Instead, take echinacea tablets or liquid.

Aromatic Solutions

Essential oils are ideal for the treatment of colds and flu as they work at the deepest level to strengthen immunity. In this way they build resistance to infection or, if infection is already present, gently ease symptoms, lessen the risk of secondary bacterial infection and speed recovery. All the oils listed below may be used in the aromatherapeutic treatment of colds and flu.

Oils for Colds and Flu

Oil	Eases Symptoms	Anti-bacterial	Immune Stimulant
Bergamot		*	*
Eucalyptus	*	*	*
Lavender	*	*	*
Lemon	*	*	*
Myrtle	*	*	*
Niaouli	*	*	*
Ravansara		* +	*
Rosemary	*	*	
Sandalwood		*	
Tea tree	*	* +	*
Thyme-linalol	*	*	

+ Tea tree and ravansara also have anti-viral properties.

Lavender is especially beneficial for aches and pains, eucalyptus or myrtle for congestion and catarrh, marjoram and lavender for headaches, niaouli for coughs, and rosemary or thyme for fatigue. Lavender and marjoram are sedating oils and therefore good in night-time cold remedies; rosemary and thyme are stimulating oils if you need to fortify youself for a busy day ahead.

Prevention
If a family member is ill or if the flu has hit your workplace, an essential oil blend vaporised in an aromatic

burner or bowl, or a few drops on a radiator, can help to
purify the air and strengthen your resistance.

Cold and Flu Resistance Builders	
Aromatic Burner	*Massage Blend*
2 drops bergamot	3 teaspoons sweet almond
1 drop thyme	2 drops sandalwood
or	1 drop lavender
1 drop eucalyptus	1 drop ravansara
2–3 drops lemon	1–2 drops myrtle

Use the above blend, not only for a back massage but
also to rub into your chest and around your nose for
added protection. To fight off quickly the first signs of a
cold or flu, prepare the massage blend and apply it to your
chest, neck, upper arms and upper back, then jump into a
comfortably hot bath and soak for ten to fifteen minutes.
Dry yourself quickly, put on cotton night clothes and
jump into bed. This is a very powerful method of dealing
with a cold or flu, as the essential oils are forced into the
body by the heat of the water. Sweating will occur during
the night, allowing toxins to be eliminated (hence the
necessity of wearing cotton rather than synthetic fab-
rics), and the body is helped to fight the virus. This
treatment has been known to clear up a bad cold or
the onset of flu literally overnight.

Treatment
At the first signs of a cold, gargle with four drops of tea
tree or 2 drops of lemon and 2 drops of ravansara in a
glass of warm water. These essences can also be combined
in bath water to which I add four drops of myrtle for an
uplifting morning bath or 4 drops of lavender for a
soothing night-time bath.

Steam inhalation with essential oils is particularly
effective for colds and flu, as the steam itself helps clear
congested passageways (see p.119 for technique).

Essential Oils for Steam Inhalation

Add to a bowl of hot (not boiling) water:
1 drop myrtle
2 drops lavender
or
2 drops thyme
1 drop tea tree

This technique can be repeated two or three times a day, and can be combined with vaporising essential oils in an aromatic burner.

If your neck muscles are sore, several drops of neat lavender may be massaged into the area. You can also use a massage blend to decongest the nose or chest, or to ease coughing. While not all aromatherapists agree with using essential oils internally, I treat ticklish coughs and sore throats with a cough mixture prepared from one drop of niaouli mixed well with one teaspoon of honey. Small amounts of this may be taken two hourly for a ticklish cough, and often provide fast and gentle relief.

Massage Blend for Congestion

2 teaspoons sweet almond
1 drop thyme-linalol
1 drop niaouli
or
2 drops lemon
1 drop tea tree
in 2 teaspoons sweet almond

Massage Blend for Cough Relief

2 teaspoons sweet almond
1 drop niaouli
2 drops sandalwood
3 drops lavender

Other Alternatives

Homeopathy, vitamin therapy, applied Kiniesiology, reflexology.

Concentration Lacking

The ability to focus our minds for clear, creative thought is dependent on us being free from distracting internal 'noise'. Worries that play like never-ceasing refrains, or deeper anxieties that cause confusion, agitation and restlessness, prevent us concentrating on the task in hand. Whether it's called 'not paying attention', 'easily bored and distracted', 'spaced out and forgetful' or the brand-new American syndrome 'Attention Deficit Disorder' or ADD, the root cause is the same: stress and its consequent anxiety. Therefore any attempt to increase the ability to concentrate in yourself or your children must address possible stressful events and ways of coping with them, as well as strategies to reduce the attendant ANXIETY. Like a seesaw, the lower the level of anxiety, the higher the level of concentration – and vice versa.

General Guidelines

In children especially, specific physical reasons for inattentiveness must first be looked for. Can the child see the blackboard? Can he hear the teachers? Does he have any physical discomfort that is distracting him? Is he intellectually under-challenged, or are the tasks beyond his capabilities? Could there be a food allergy which is causing the problem? Medical research is now saying that ADD (see Useful Addresses) is often linked to hyperactivity, and that both problems could be markedly helped with careful attention to diet and the avoidance of food additives such as dyes and preservatives. For children in whom concentration is a persistent and troubling problem, consulting an educational psychologist may elicit some practical and comforting advice. Threatening a child with punishment obviously only increases his stress – and his inability to concentrate.

Adults can suffer when trying to cope with too many tasks at a time, and it becomes easy to drift from one task to another without completing anything satisfactorily. A simple recommendation is to write a list of all the things which must be done/accomplished, whether it be a phone call to make, a letter to write, tax return to complete, a party to organise and so on (see Chapter 5). This has the remarkable effect of lightening the mental load by lessening both stress and anxiety.

Aromatic Solutions

While tackling the underlying issues, several essential oils may be used to increase concentration and stimulate the mind; these include basil, peppermint, rosemary and thyme. Of these, rosemary is my favourite for its distinctive, pleasing aroma and romantic associations with antiquity. It is said that students in ancient Greece wore wreaths of rosemary, and Shakespeare too proclaimed its powers: 'There's rosemary, that's for remembrance.'

Whenever lack of concentration is due to stress, inhale deeply the scent of rosemary or vaporise six drops of this mentally stimulating essential oil in an aromatic burner. I sometimes add three drops of lemon, which is uplifting, and two drops of geranium to harmonise and stabilise the emotions. These three oils may also be combined with a base oil and gently massaged into the temples or behind the neck (see p. 132 for technique).

Oils to Help with Concentration		
	Antidepressant	Mental Stimulant
Basil	*	
Black pepper		*
Eucalyptus		*
Grapefruit	*	*
Lemon		*
Lemongrass	*	*
Palmarosa		*
Peppermint		*
Rosemary	*	*
Rosewood	*	*
Spike lavender	*	*
Tea tree		*
Thyme-linalol		*

Other Alternatives

Bach flower remedies, homeopathy, hypnotherapy, McTimony chiropractic, NLP, Psychotherapy, reflexology, vitamin therapy.

Constipation

No body function is more personal or more individual than defecation. Despite the widespread myth that daily bowel movements are essential for good health, normal defecation varies from three times a day to once every three days. However, as a result of this incorrect assumption many people over-use suppositories, enemas and laxatives, producing a real problem where originally there was only an imagined one. Constipation is truly best defined by you, for only you know when defecation is difficult or infrequent according to your natural pattern.

When it does occur, constipation may signal mechanical obstruction, a tumour, diverticulitis, malfunction of the hormonal glands, or an inactive, lazy colon which is typical in elderly people. If you are concerned, consult your doctor. However, one of the most frequent and often under-considered causes of constipation is stress. Some experts claim that constipation reflects a way of holding on to old, often suppressed hurts, while others maintain that it is an attempt to gain control over an otherwise uncontrollable situation such as a stressful, over-demanding work schedule.

General Guidelines

I recommend staying away from, or getting off, all laxatives, and giving the colon the chance to rediscover how to function on its own. If the constipation is due to stress, it may be wise to set aside some time every day (fifteen to twenty minutes after breakfast, for example) for this function. We all feel rushed and hurried when under stress, but not having the time for a bowel movement is surely a sign that one's priorities are askew.

I am sure you are aware of the need to drink plenty of water or healthy liquids every day, and to eat lots of roughage. High-fibre foods, such as raw vegetables, fresh fruit and whole grains, encourage intestinal peristalsis – the muscular action which pushes food through the gut. Fats, dairy products, refined sugars and starches all increase the likelihood of constipation, while red meat, which takes several days to digest, may aggravate it. Inactivity and a sedentary lifestyle are also associated with constipation, and regular exercise is recommended.

If you have haemorrhoids (piles) as a result of over-straining, there are several gentle yoga exercises that help strengthen the abdominal and rectal muscles. Haemorrhoids usually cause bright red painless bleeding during a bowel movement, and are not a dangerous condition. But do consult your doctor if you have rectal bleeding, as it may signal an underlying problem that requires immediate attention.

Aromatic Solutions

Massage of the abdomen and lower back (see pages 99–132 for techniques) with a blend of essential oils for fifteen or twenty minutes every morning helps to stimulate bowel function.

Massage Blend for Constipation
50 ml base oil, e.g. sweet almond 20 drops marjoram 5 drops rose *or* geranium   *or* 5 drops peppermint 15 drops lemon

Massaging the buttocks (see p. 101) can also stimulate a bowel movement. Although this area will feel tender, massage it for a few minutes each day.

If you have haemorrhoids, either take a sitz bath (see below) or use compresses soaked in aromatic water twice a day.

Essential Oils for Haemorrhoids (Sitz bath)
Add any of the following to a bowl or bidet of comfortably warm water: 10 drops cypress *or* 6 drops frankincense *or* 6 drops myrtle *or* 4 drops patchouli *or* 6 drops juniper *or* 4 drops lavender and 2 drops geranium

Other Alternatives

Homeopathy, cranio-sacral therapy, McTimony chiropractic, reflexology, shiatsu, vitamin therapy.

Cystitis

In cystitis an inflammation of the bladder caues a frequent urge to urinate; the small amounts of urine passed are often accompanied by a burning pain. Blood in the urine or fever accompanying cystitis must always be reported to a doctor. The infection is bacterial in origin and usually spreads to the urethra via contamination from the intestinal tract, or by minor trauma to the urinary tract caused by repeated sexual intercourse (thus its common name, honeymoon cystitis).

The infection is far more frequent in women than men, as the female urethra is shorter and closer to the anus. Pregnant women and those on oral contraceptives are especially prone to cystitis as these conditions affect the hormonal system, which in turn alters the natural bacterial flora in the urethra. Persistent cystitis may result from repeated use of antibiotics that not only lower immune function (see IMMUNE DEFICIENCY) but also disturb the balance of intestinal bacteria. Antibiotics may, however, be necessary to prevent the spread of infection to the kidneys; the decision must be a personal one, reflecting your belief in these drugs as well as the severity of the problem.

For many of us, cystitis, especially if it is a recurrent problem, is our individual response to stress and a manifestation of its effects on the immune system. In addition, since the muscles of the urethra and the bladder itself are not isolated from other muscles in the body, they react to stress by contraction and spasm in exactly the same way as the back or neck muscles. The aromatic oils are particularly effective for cystitis as they work not just to combat bacteria, which they do superbly, but also to relax the whole person and in this way reduce constriction, spasm and pain in affected areas. Several of the essential oils also encourage urination, which subsequently eases the flow and speeds the removal of toxins.

General Guidelines

Drink lots of water or cranberry juice, which will help reduce inflammation and pain and remove unwanted organisms. Diuretic herbal teas or soothing camomile tea should be substituted for coffee, tea or alcohol, which will exacerbate the problem. Similarly, strong, spicy foods and those high in refined sugar are best avoided, as are vaginal deodorants, bubble baths or any other chemical irritants. The advice to abstain from sex is probably unnecessary, as this is usually the last thing on a woman's mind. Loose-fitting clothing and cotton undergarments that allow the skin to breathe fully are the most comfortable, and also lessen the heat and humidity on which bacteria thrive.

Aromatic Solutions

Many essential oils are effective in the treatment of cystitis and can be used either alone or, if necessary, in conjunction with antibiotics.

Essential Oils for Cystitis

Oil	Antibacterial	Antispasmodic	Increases Urination	Calming
Bergamot	*	*		*
Camomile	*			*
Juniper	*		*	
Lavender	*	*		*
Marjoram	*	*		*
Niaouli	*			
Rosemary	*	*	*	
Sandalwood	*	*		*
Thyme-linalol	*	*		

Massage of the lower abdomen and lower back, particularly the kidney region (see p. 99 for technique), once
daily will provide relief in a few days. Use five drops of
sandalwood in 10ml base oil, because it has a special
affinity for the genito-urinary tract, or use three drops of
juniper with two drops of camomile to promote the flow of
urine and lessen inflammation.

A sitz bath with lavender is also very soothing, especially when used in conjunction with massage. Just add
ten drops of lavender to a bowl large enough to sit in, or
to two inches of comfortable but cool bath water, mix
thoroughly and soak for ten minutes or so. If this is not
convenient, a cotton wool pad soaked in lavender water
(one drop lavender in 100ml water, shaken well before
each use) can be used to cleanse the vulva after urinating.

If you are prone to repeated cystitis, daily bathing with
essential oils to increase your general resistance as well
as to control bacterial build-up is highly recommended.
Any of the oils listed can be used alone or in a combination to suit your preference.

Other Alternatives

Homeopathy, reflexology, vitamin therapy.

Depression

Like a black cloud obscuring the sun, depression may
happen to any of us given enough stress for enough time.
While the symptoms of depression may feel very frightening, in reality the condition is no more than a state of
profound emotional fatigue – an inability to carry our
burden, whether internal or external, any longer (see
FATIGUE). Sometimes a state of depression can arise
because of an inner conflict – when we go against our

intuition and do something we know we shouldn't do; conversely, when we are not doing something which we know we should be doing we can also become very depressed.

Those who admonish us just to get on with things misjudge the full weight of depression, and more importantly miss seeing the constructive opportunity that this condition offers. However bleak you may feel, depression may in fact mark the beginning of a new freedom. To paraphrase an old proverb, trouble should be like a tunnel we go through, at the end of which there is understanding, the possibility for change and release from issues that constrain us. Your depression is nature's way of saying that there are issues that must be dealt with – a kindly force pushing you through the dark tunnel, to the light and freedom at the other side.

Some Symptoms of Depression
Fearfulness Loss of appetite Reduced sexual drive Sense of unworthiness Guilt Irritability Insomnia and other sleep problems Loss of confidence Hopelessness Suicidal thoughts Indecisiveness Anxiety Fear of illness Paranoia

General Guidelines

Often we cannot – and need not – do it alone. There are so many people who can help, from friends and family to professional counsellors, that suffering alone and in silence is not necessary. The way forward often lies in the support and compassion of others and in open dialogue from which we can learn and grow.

We can break up a pattern of negative thoughts about ourselves by the use of an affirmation. An affirmation is a phrase which is repeated every morning, afternoon and evening, until we start to believe it is true. An excellent affirmation for anyone who is depressed is: 'I like myself unconditionally, knowing that I improve every day in every way.'

Until the pain has passed, however, there are some practical things you can do to speed the process. Although you may need a sanctuary for a while, in general it is best to keep occupied, preferably at a task you enjoy. Go out into the daylight to see the beauty of a flower or feel the wind. Visit friends and listen to their troubles: giving to others feels good and may distract you from your own cares. Walk, exercise and use your physical body, which will benefit from the release of the chemical onslaught caused by your emotions. Eat, if you can, your favourite healthy foods. Listen to lovely music and allow moments of pleasure into the gloom. A happy experience each day, no matter how small, can start a new positive cycle of relaxation and relief. Think a comforting thought instead of a despairing one. Substitute hope and faith for despair, keep a vision of what you can be, will be, clearly in focus; then be patient, and wait until you reach the end of the tunnel.

Aromatic Solutions

For me, there is no lovelier way to bring the sunshine back into life than aromatherapy. Because the aroma of the essential oils is transported via the olfactory nerve directly to that area of the brain which controls our moods and emotions (see Chapter 3), the oils can profoundly affect how we think and feel. Pure essential oils have powers over us that are as diverse as our needs for them: not just one oil for depression, but many, each for a different variation of depression.

Depression with Anxiety
Bergamot
Clary sage
Frankincense
Melissa
Rosewood
Verbena

Depression with Apathy and Despair
Black pepper
Clary Sage
Eucalyptus
Juniper
Orange
Palmarosa
Sandalwood
Verbena

Depression with Guilt
Bergamot Clary sage Geranium Juniper Lavender Sandalwood Ylang-ylang

Depression with Irritability
Jasmine Myrtle Patchouli Sandalwood

Depression with Insomnia
Angelica Geranium Lavender Marjoram Melissa Ylang-ylang

The essential oils listed above may be used alone or in combinations of two or three. Personal smell preference should be the guiding factor, as your body will often instinctively choose what it most needs. The oils are easily used at home, either in an aromatic burner (two to four drops in water), daily baths (six to ten drops to a full bath), or inhaled directly from the bottle. A professional aromatherapy massage adds the healing power of touch and is highly recommended, but if it is not possible for you to obtain one then a daily massage of your temples, neck and solar plexus (see pages 132, 104 and 109) is a soothing substitute. Several of my favourite anti-depression formulas are given here.

Essential Oils in Aromatic Burner for Depression with Anxiety

1–2 drops frankincense
1–2 drops clary sage
1–2 drops bergamot

Bath Oils for Depression with Irritability

To a full bath of water, add:
3–4 drops myrtle
2 drops ylang-ylang
4 drops lavender

Massage Blend for Depression with Despair

2 teaspoons sweet almond
1 drop jasmine
2 drops palmarosa
3–4 drops sandalwood

Other Alternatives

Acupuncture, Bach flower remedies, cranio-sacral therapy, homeopathy, NLP, shiatsu, hypnotherapy, psychotherapy, reflexology.

Diarrhoea

As discussed under CONSTIPATION, diarrhoea can only be defined relative to your own particular pattern of bowel movement. Frequent or loose stools may be normal for you, or conversely may be a symptom of an underlying disorder. There are many possible causes of diarrhoea: lactose intolerance, drug therapy, malabsorption of nutrients by the intestinal wall, or mucosal diseases such as ulcerative colitis. But generally most cases of diarrhoea are the result of bacterial or viral infection; food intolerance or poisoning; or stress and anxiety — the so-called nervous diarrhoea. The mechanisms by which anxiety leads to diarrhoea are complex, but hormonal factors certainly play a role. It is known, for example, that high levels of the chemical mood regulator serotonin stimulate intestinal smooth muscle and thus speed the passage of waste through the gut.

General Guidelines

The first line of attack is to replace lost fluids. Diarrhoea can lead quickly to dehydration, and it is crucial to drink large quantities of cool liquid. If the diarrhoea is extensive or long-term, it is important to seek medical advice. Alternatively, when travelling abroad you may wish to take a commercial preparation to replace the sodium, potassium and magnesium which may have been lost along with the fluid. You can also make your own mixture:

Anti-dehydration Drink
1 litre bottled water 1 teaspoon baking soda 4 teaspoons sugar and the juice of a fresh lemon *or* 8 drops lemon essential oil

Irritating foods should be avoided, but it is always best to follow your body's advice and eat what it craves.

Aromatic Solutions

A warm bath with added oils of geranium and/or neroli is most soothing and steadying when stress has caused a bowel upset. But other oils, such as lemon, sandalwood and lavender, may also be used. If you have diarrhoea accompanied by colic or flatulence, then camomile or peppermint compresses are very helpful (see p. 155).

During an acute attack of diarrhoea, it is advisable to massage the entire abdomen using gentle circular movements.

Massage Blends for Diarrhoea	
2 teaspoons sweet almond	2 teaspoons sweet almond
1 drop geranium	3 drops neroli
2 drops camomile *or*	2 drops lemon
2 drops sandalwood	1 drop peppermint

Alternatively, use these oils in warm water instead of base oil to make a gentle compress for the abdomen.

Other Alternatives

Applied kinesiology, homeopathy, NLP, reflexology, vitamin therapy.

Dysmenorrhoea

Painful menstruation in a young girl who has just begun her periods (primary dysmenorrhoea) is thought to be associated with hormonal imbalances, physiological development or psychological factors. Fears and anxiety about her unfolding sexuality and embarrassment with her changing body may be reflected by an intensified, painful response to menstruation. When dysmenorrhoea occurs in later life (secondary dysmenorrhoea) it is, however, sometimes associated with specific infectious or anatomical causes, such as fibroids, pelvic inflammatory disease or endometriosis. In both primary and secondary dysmenorrhoea, painful periods are aggravated by emotional factors and stress. Although the mechanism is still unclear, it appears that stress exacerbates uterine muscle contraction and spasm and constricts the blood vessels, thus obstructing the flow of blood through the cervix.

The pain of dysmenorrhoea is cramp-like and may be located in the lower abdomen, thighs or back. It may be present only at the onset of menstruation or persist for the duration of the period. In some women nausea, diarrhoea, increased frequency of urination, headache and painful breasts may be associated complaints, as may – not surprisingly – irritability and depression.

Painful periods, especially when caused or aggravated by stress, are particularly amenable to treatment with essential oils. The oils act immediately to lift the pain and depression, and, over time, to regulate the smooth functioning of this natural process.

General Guidelines

Menstruation is not an ailment to be cured, but one of a woman's greatest glories as it signals her capacity to conceive. This may seem like an over-romanticised view, and yet if we opened ourselves up to this process, rather than fearing and dreading it, I suspect much monthly pain would cease.

Until we achieve this ideal state of receptivity, however, reassurance and support of your teenage daughter may be required, as may some gentle words of wisdom to yourself. Of course, severe or persistent period pain needs to be checked out by a physician.

Aromatic Solutions

Numerous essential oils may be used in the treatment of dysmenorrhoea. Some are relaxing, for when you feel uptight and tense; others are uplifting, for when you feel heavy and depressed. Yet others (called emmenagogues) increase the menstrual flow and may be used if relief comes with greater flow; these are, of course, best avoided if your period is already too heavy. Some oils reduce spasm and cramps, while others work over a period of time to regulate the hormonal system.

Essential Oils for Dysmenorrhoea

Oil	Relaxing	Uplifting	Increase Flow	Antispasmodic	Hormone Regulator
Angelica		*		*	*
Camomile	*			*	
Clary sage	*	*	*	*	*
Geranium	*	*			*
Lavender	*			*	
Marjoram	*			*	
Melissa	*			*	*
Rose	*	*		*	*
Thyme-linalol		*	*	*	
Verbena	*	*		*	

Clary sage is my favourite oil for painful periods as it brings almost instant relief from pain and discomfort and, being a euphoric oil, takes the 'curse' out of menstruation. As a teenager I suffered from dysmenorrhoea; it persisted until I was well into my twenties, and I was only free of it after discovering the wonders of aromatherapy and, in particular, clary sage. If your period is heavy but the pain is not lessened by the flow, choose one of the antispasmodic oils such as geranium, melissa or rose. Rose is called the queen of oils for good reason, as this sublime scent is one of the best essences for 'female' problems of all sorts. When you are having a particularly painful period, an aromatherapy massage of the lower back and abdomen, directly above the pubic hair line, offers rapid relief from pain. The area should be massaged a day or two before your period is due and continued for as long as you feel discomfort.

Massage Blends for Dysmenorrhoea	
2 teaspoons sweet almond 1 drop angelica 1 drop geranium 3 drops lavender	*or*

2 teaspoons sweet almond 3 drops clary sage 1 drop geranium 1 drop camomile *or* melissa

Hot compresses using these essential oils may also be applied directly to the painful area, left in place for fifteen minutes, and renewed as often as necessary. Many women opt for quick showers during menstruation, but if you prefer to have a bath, add to comfortably warm water six to ten drops of clary sage or three drops of each oil from the above list (minus sweet almond).

My preferred method of treating period pains is to take two drops of clary sage in a teaspoon of honey with a little hot water. Usually one dose at the beginning of the period, when the pain is at its worst, is all that is required – but a second dose may be taken a few hours later if necessary.

Other Alternatives

Acupuncture, applied Kiniesiology, cranio-sacral therapy, homeopathy, McTimony chiropractic, reflexology, Shiatsu.

Eczema

The term literally means 'to boil over', which well describes this painful condition with flaky red skin that itches and weeps. Eczema, like asthma and hay fever is associated with an inherited allergy, and often flares up during times of stress. The way it manifests itself, and its underlying causes, are very varied. Atopic eczema, perhaps the most common, is usually worse in the creases of the elbows, knees and wrists, but may also be seen on the face, neck and trunk. The condition may start shortly after birth, and clears up by the age of ten in 90 per cent of children. If a particular area is constantly scratched or irritated it ultimately becomes thickened, with a well-demarcated ridge of purple skin. This disorder, called lichenified eczema, is found especially in over-stressed individuals. Alternatively, there may be a dull grey, cracking, ulcerated patch around the ankles; this is known as varicose eczema.

General Guidelines

It is very important to determine the allergens – such as household chemicals, cosmetics or certain foods – that cause or aggravate the condition and to eliminate them wherever possible. Stress is involved in almost all cases of eczema, however, and it is important to reduce the level of emotional strain; see Chapter 5 for guidelines on lessening stress, including aromatic baths and adding essences to the air. Remember that children with eczema may be picking up on adult tensions, so both parents and offspring may need aromatic relaxation.

Some experts believe that eczema is a healthy attempt by the body to rid itself of toxins or underlying disease, and that suppressing it with powerful treatments such as steroid creams only forces the system to take these toxins further inward. It is not unusual to see children who have been 'cured' of their eczema suddenly develop asthma. I am a great believer, therefore, in the homeopathic treatment of this disorder, and have seen amazing results. Although the skin problem may get temporarily worse under homeopathic treatment as the body throws off its wastes, permanent safe cures can be achieved in this way.

Aromatic Solutions

Two of the most useful essential oils for eczema are camomile and lavender, diluted in a light jojoba base. Other oils such as melissa, bergamot, neroli and rose may also be combined into a base that is applied to the affected area three times daily. As each case of eczema is unique, some experimentation may be necessary to find the essential oil best suited to you and your skin. However, if your skin (or that of a child) is very sensitive, use only diluted lavender for bathing the affected area.

Eczema Blend		
15ml jojoba	or	15ml sweet almond
2 drops camomile		1 drop rose
1 drop bergamot		2 drops geranium
4 drops lavender		4 drops sandalwood

If the eczema is weepy or inflamed, two drops of patchouli may be added to the formula above.

To relieve the sometimes intolerable itch of eczema, a few drops of camomile and lavender can be used in a cold compress for the skin or a soothing bath. Lavender is particularly recommended as it soothes, heals and encourages the growth of healthy new skin.

Other Alternatives

Acupuncture, Bach flower remedies, cranio-sacral therapy, homeopathy, hypnotherapy, vitamin therapy.

Fatigue

There are two types of fatigue. One is a healthy fatigue, in which the body requires rest and replenishment; after a good nights' sleep. fatigue is replaced by vitality. Very little effort is necessary on your part other than putting your head on the pillow. The other is a more diffuse fatigue which signals that your system is in overload. This type of mental fatigue is familiar to us all at some time and to some degree, and is always due to stress. It is a tiredness that demotivates us and makes even simple tasks a struggle; it robs us of our patience, our humour, our sense of perspective and even our sleep. This is a punishing fatigue that requires a conscious act of will to overcome. For while the solution is clearly to stop and let the mind and emotions rest, an overwrought system often needs help to do just that. It is here that the essential oils show their brilliance as one of nature's greatest healers.

General Guidelines

A few simple changes to your lifestyle can make a big difference to your fatigue level. No system can function without fuel, and proper nutrition is vital. The natural tendency may be to reach for stimulants – coffee, tea, sugar – but these are inevitably followed by a crash back to fatigue. Healthy foods and vitamins, not eaten on the run but consumed slowly during a real break in the day, are step number one towards feeling better.

In addition, although you may feel exhausted, exercise is marvellous for nervous fatigue. Not only does it help tire out your body, but strenuous exercise releases endorphins that create an overall sense of wellbeing that dispels the heaviness of fatigue. If no other form of exercise is possible, walk vigorously in the fresh air, breathing deeply to fill your system with cleansing oxygen.

Since your fatigue is stress-related, no true improvement can take place until the underlying stress is lessened. Mental fatigue requires mental rest.

Aromatic Solutions

Mental fatigue develops over a long stressful period, and requires commitment and patience to resolve. The process towards rebuilding energy and vitality will occur slowly as the system is gradually unwound and de-stressed.

Stage 1: Oils to Calm and Relax	
Camomile	Marjoram
Geranium	Neroli
Lavender	Vetivert

Stage 2: Oils to Balance and Uplift	
Bergamot	Geranium
Clary sage	Orange
Frankincense	Rosewood

Stage 3: Oils to Build Energy and Stamina	
Basil	Peppermint
Black pepper	Rosemary
Grapefruit	Thyme-linalol

Stage 4: Oils to Inspire	
Cedarwood	Rose
Frankincense	Sandalwood
Jasmine	

As an inhalation, breathe deeply from the bottle or simply add a few drops to a bowl of hot water or an aromatic burner.

As a bath oil, add a few drops of the chosen essential oils to a warm bath and agitate the water.

As a compress for the head, eyes or solar plexus, place a few drops of essential oil in water before dipping a cloth into it.

As a massage oil for head, neck, shoulders, back, solar plexus or wherever you feel tension, use 1 teaspoon of base oil (roughly 5 ml) with two to three drops of essential oil (see p. 99 for technique).

As a perfume dabbed behind the ears or on the wrists, use ten drops of your favourite essential oils in 10ml of jojoba.

Alternatively, add ten drops to 100ml distilled or pure bottled water to create a lovely healing cologne.

Other Alternatives

Acupuncture, Bach flower remedies, cranio-sacral therapy, homeopathy, McTimony chiropractic, NLP, Psychotherapy, reflexology.

Flu

See COLDS AND FLU.

Frozen Shoulder

See SHOULDER PAIN.

Haemorrhoids

See CONSTIPATION.

Halitosis

Other than poor oral hygiene, the most typical causes of bad breath are digestive problems, respiratory infections and tooth decay or gum disease. But halitosis also often occurs at times of great physical and emotional stress – perhaps, like a porcupine's needles, to keep the world at bay.

General Guidelines

If your bad breath is persistent and its cause is not clear, it is probably wise to consult your doctor or dentist. But if you notice that halitosis occurs during periods of intense worry or before a stressful event, some of the general guidelines in Chapter 5 may help clear up the underlying problem rather than simply masking one of its manifestations.

Frequently drink an adequate amount of pure water. You can't expect your body to flush away toxins which occur when under stress, if you deprive your body of water. Proper nutrition is essential, so eat wisely instead of snacking, and from time to time, eat those foods which give a pleasant smell to the breath:– parsley, mint and raw celery.

Aromatic Solutions

Several aromatic oils, including peppermint, lemon, clary sage, tea tree, bergamot, niaouli and rose, can easily be made into a fragrant mouthwash that not only tastes pleasant but also kills bacteria. If you use distilled or pure bottled water and a dark tightly stoppered bottle, an aromatic mouthwash will last for several weeks.

Aromatic Mouthwash		
200 ml water	*or*	200ml water
1 drop peppermint		1 drop tea-tree
1 drop lemon		2 drops bergamot

Also see section on TENSION.

Other Alternatives

Applied Kiniesiology, Bach flower remedies, homeopathy, reflexology, vitamin therapy.

Headaches and Migraine

Headaches are one of the most common complaints with which doctors have to deal, and for the most part they are related to stress and anxiety. Although the pain is not life-threatening, it can bring sustained misery and dread to the sufferer's life.

A headache generally starts in one place, commonly the base of the skull, and spreads until the whole head is affected. It may be throbbing, or may feel like a tight band around the head. Many headaches are brought on by nervous tension which affects the muscles of the shoulders, neck and head, setting up a physical tension which causes pain, which in turn leads to more tension being created – so forming a vicious circle.

Migraines differ from headaches in that they are much more debilitating. The pain is often excruciating and can be accompanied by NAUSEA, aversion to light, dizziness and noise intolerance. A typical migraine starts with what is called the prodroma – the period prior to the migraine proper, which encompasses irritability, high or low moods, obsessional behaviour, and difficulty in thinking, speaking or concentrating. This is usually followed by what is termed the aura – visual disturbances and neurological symptoms – and then by onset of acute pain.

The frequency and severity of migraines varies from one individual to another, but most sufferers relate their onset to times of stress.

General Guidelines

For your own peace of mind it is wise to visit your doctor and check that your headaches have no organic cause. An eye test is also advisable, as straining to focus can bring on headaches.

For people who are certain that their headache/migraine is not a sign of more serious illness, painkilling tablets are generally recommended, but these do nothing to help the underlying tension. Relaxation exercises are a more direct and permanent way to combat tension and bring relief. Taking time to learn such techniques is a positive step towards breaking the chain of tension and pain. Hot or cold compresses also may be of help.

Some sufferers find that fluorescent lighting, PMT or the contraceptive pill precipitate or worsen an attack. It is important to get to know your own body and its reactions, in order to identify and monitor your own particular stressors. All migraine sufferers should look at their diet, as food can be a trigger. Chocolate, cheese, alcohol and citrus fruits are common culprits, but not the only ones. Caffeine, monosodium glutamate and various other foods can precipitate an attack in some people, so it is sensible to keep a 'food diary' until the pattern of your migraines is uncovered.

Aromatic Solutions

Aromatic baths and massage to release tension and lessen feelings of being 'stressed out' are helpful in the long-term treatment of headaches and migraine.

Bath Oils
Choose from any of the oils in this list, or blend, two together to make your own special bath fragrance:
Bergamot Clary sage Frankincense Geranium Lavender Lemon Marjoram Melissa Neroli Orange Rosewood Ylang-ylang

Massage Blends for Headache or Migraine
15ml sweet almond 1 drop vetivert 2 drops sandalwood 2 drops ylang-ylang 1 drop geranium   *or* 10ml sweet almond 2 drops lavender 4 drops neroli

At the onset of a tension headache, take a little lavender oil on the tips of your fingers and massage it into the top of the neck/base of the skull. Very often this treatment can prevent a headache from developing, and when used to treat a severe headache it will often reduce the pain within half an hour.

If tension has also interfered with your digestion you will have a sick headache. The fastest cure for this is a cup of peppermint water (see p. 212). Sipped slowly over ten minutes, this remedy is little short of miraculous.

A migraine sufferer may not be able to tolerate a neck massage, as any movement is liable to worsen the symptoms. Instead, drop a tiny amount of basil oil onto one fingertip and lightly rub it into the temples. Alternatively, the anxiety and distress generated by the pain may be relieved by lying in a darkened room. First, however, place a drop or two of a relaxing/calming essential oil in a bowl of hot water or a candle fragancer. Ideal essences for use are bergamot, cypress, frankincense, geranium, lavender, marjoram, melissa, neroli, orange, patchouli, rosemary, rosewood, ylang-ylang. Since all migraine sufferers feel very delicate and are highly sensitive to aromas during an attack, only use an essence which is liked.

Other Alternatives

Acupuncture, applied kinesiology, cranio-sacral therapy, homeopathy, hypnotherapy, McTimony chiropractic, NLP, psychotherapy, reflexology, vitamin therapy.

See also NECK PAIN, SHOULDER PAIN.

Heart Attack

See RECOVERY FROM HEART ATTACK.

Herpes

The common viral infection known as herpes simplex is characterised by small, fluid-filled blisters. In most cases the infection is mild, but for some sufferers the condition can be very distressing; for people with already depressed immune systems, such as those with AIDS, the virus may even prove to be life-threatening.

The virus is of two main types – HSV1 (herpes 1) which affects the face, especially the lips, and HSV2 (herpes 2), which usually affects the genitals. With HSV1 the initial illness is often flu-like and there may be mouth ulcers as well as large blisters on the lips. Subsequently the virus remains in the nerve cells of the face and periodically breaks out into cold sores, usually when the sufferer has a cold or fever or is feeling run down and generally suffering from stress.

HSV2 is sexually transmitted, and common symptoms are itching, burning blisters in the genital area, which burst to become painful ulcers. The sufferer may feel generally unwell, and women may find urination very painful.

General Guidelines

In the case of genital herpes, bathing the area with a solution of one heaped teaspoon of salt to half a litre of water can help ease the itching and pain and keep the area clean. Sexual activity should be avoided until the symptoms have disappeared, since both types of herpes simplex are contagious.

Women should avoid wearing tight pants or jeans and try to use only cotton underwear whilst the symptoms persist. Wear stockings rather than tights so that the genital area does not get too hot and moist. Men should wear cotton boxer shorts rather than tight-fitting underwear.

Sunshine can bring on cold sores or make existing ones worse, due to changes in skin temperature and exposure to ultraviolet rays, so take care during the summer or when holidaying in a hot climate. Careful washing will help prevent the spread of infection to areas such as the eyes, where serious conjunctivitis can result.

The orthodox medical approach is to prescribe an antiviral drug which quickly heals the sores; however there is no actual cure for herpes 1 or 2, and it is wise to try to prevent a recurrence. As stress is implicated, eat a healthy, immune-strengthening diet and look for ways to limit anxiety and tension in your life (see Chapter 5).

Diet can also play its part in the maintenance of a herpes attack, as the amino acid argenine is known to make the symptoms worse. Foods that contain argenine and should therefore be avoided are sesame seeds, onions, coconut, peanuts and peanut butter, cabbage, carob, cocoa (and therefore chocolate) and several kinds of nut (macadamia, walnuts, brazil, almonds, pecans, cashews). The amino acid lysine is helpful in stimulating the body's resistance to herpes; lysine-rich foods include goat's milk, dairy products, figs, peaches, fish, poultry, dates, beans, turnips, asparagus, egg whites and spinach.

Aromatic Solutions

Immune-strengthening aromatic baths and massage are extremely helpful and can help the body to resist an outbreak of herpes.

Bath Blend
Choose any one or two from this list and add a total of 6–10 drops to a full bath of water, agitating the water well before stepping in: Bergamot Clary sage Frankincense Geranium Juniper Lavender Lemon Melissa Myrtle Niaouli Ravansara Rose Rosewood

Massage Blend
15ml sweet almond 2 drops bergamot 2 drops lavender 3 drops sandalwood 2 drops orange *or* 15ml sweet almond 2 drops ravansara 2 drops myrtle 4 drops lavender

Two essential oils are more helpful than any others in the treatment of herpes lesions – melissa, which is rare and very expensive, and tea tree, which is inexpensive and easily available. Tea tree is quite remarkable in that a little can be applied directly from the bottle to a lesion on the lips, where it has a slightly analgesic effect. During the course of a day, tea tree may be applied in this way every hour or so; if treatment is started at the first tingling feelings, it is often possible to prevent a full outbreak. Tea tree is antiviral and can inhibit the growth of the herpes virus if caught early enough; but whenever treatment with tea tree is started, the healing process is speeded up.

Genital herpes can be treated in the same way as herpes of the lips. Tea tree is a safe oil to use on the delicate mucous lining in this area of the body.

Other Alternatives

Bach flower remedies, homeopathy, reflexology, vitamin therapy.

Hypertension

High blood pressure or hypertension is extremely common and is thought to affect 20 per cent of the population. Known to shorten our lifespan, it puts considerable strain on the heart and can lead to heart failure, strokes and brain haemorrhage.

Hypertension falls into two distinct categories: the first accompanies atherosclerosis and must always be treated by a doctor because the risks of heart attack or stroke are greatly increased. However, the second type, essential hypertension, has many causes including a high fat diet, a high-salt diet, obesity, lack of exercise, smoking and, of course, stress. 'White-coat hypertension' is well documented in hospitals, as a patient's blood pressure increases when the doctor arrives.

Essential hypertension can be caused by suppressing the emotions and being unable to verbalise one's feelings. We all know people who put on a brave face and seem to be good at coping with difficulties, but who one day astonish us by admitting that they don't sleep very well because they are so wound up. Sometimes a current event will trigger off emotions from the past, and if those past emotions are not dealt with then once again a lid is put on the pot. Just as food is cooked more quickly by the pressure of trapped steam, so too do emotions boiling inside us create a state of internal hyperactivity. This condition forces through the valves of the heart more blood than can comfortably flow through at one time – hence the raising of blood pressure.

Most people's blood pressure fluctuates throughout the day, with periods of acute stress forcing it higher. Usually, when the worry is resolved it returns to normal. However, if the body is exposed to long periods of stress the result may be more permanent high blood pressure.

General Guidelines

Once the disease is present, there are recognised ways to slow down and reverse the process. Diet is vital – cut down on salt, red meat, fats and refined foods, and increase fresh fruit and vegetables, wholegrains and fish. Join a health club and begin a personal exercise plan, or work out ways to incorporate exercise into your daily routine, such as walking or cycling to work. Being overweight, smoking and drinking too much alcohol can also raise your blood pressure. Finally, your GP or practice nurse will have a wealth of information to help you recognise which particular habits may have contributed to your hypertension. For example, you may bottle up your troubles and emotions rather than expressing yourself openly. Many surgeries now run 'well man' and 'well woman' clinics which focus on maintaining and improving health.

Aromatic Solutions

Lavender is the most popular essential oil for reducing blood pressure, and is so effective that people with low blood pressure are always advised to avoid it. Other oils which help to lower blood pressure are marjoram, neroli and ylang-ylang. Any of them may be used in massage, in the bath, in a room fragrancer or even sniffed straight from the bottle when other methods are inconvenient or inappropriate.

A massage with neroli is highly effective in reducing the bodily and mental tensions which contribute to raised blood pressure. For this reason I strongly recommend anyone with high blood pressure to have a neroli massage before a visit to the dentist or doctor, and most especially before an operation. Anaesthesia entails a risk for any of us, but is particularly dangerous to those with high blood pressure. Other essential oils which are relaxing/sedative include bergamot, camomile, frankincense, geranium, rose and sandalwood.

High blood pressure is often accompanied by fluid retention, and any prescribed drug for the treatment of hypertension is invariably a diuretic. As an alternative to chemical diuretics, many essential oils have diuretic properties and may be used in massage. It is best to seek professional help from a qualified aromatherapist for this condition, but you may also like to consider giving your partner a massage containing oils of grapefruit, juniper, lemongrass, lemon and orange. Massage the back, the hands, the feet or the shoulders (see p. 99).

Massage Blend for Hypertension

15ml sweet almond *or* equivalent base oil
2 drops lemongrass
3 drops grapefruit
1 drop orange
    or
15ml sweet almond
2 drops juniper
3 drops grapefruit
1 drop orange

Other Alternatives

Acupuncture, applied kinesiology, cranio-sacral therapy, hypnotherapy, reflexology, vitamin therapy.

Hyperventilation

As its name suggests, hyperventilation means that the lungs are moving more air in and out of the chest than the body requires. Short-term over-breathing which is fast and shallow is a normal reaction to stress, and forms part of the fight-or-flight reaction when the body is on red alert. When the danger has passed, breathing and heart rates usually return to their resting rhythm. However, for some people over-breathing becomes a habit. Prolonged anxiety serves to heighten their breathing to the point where they experience dizziness, pins and needles, icy-cold hands and feet, erratic heartbeats and other symptoms which together can cause the sufferer to feel that he or she is in danger of dying. The vital balance between oxygen and carbon dioxide in the body has been upset and, as the body becomes more alkaline, nerve cells react against the change. The usual emergency treatment for an acute attack is to breathe into a paper bag, thus reinhaling carbon dioxide and restoring the oxygen/carbon dioxide balance.

General Guidelines

When we breathe naturally, the stomach should expand first, the upper chest movement should be limited and we should take the air in through our nose. Making time to observe our own pattern of breathing is the first step towards a return to normal breathing. As hyperventilation is now a well-recognised condition, many alternative health professionals have experience in helping sufferers back towards optimum health through the use of breathing and posture exercises, Alexander Technique and counselling. Yoga in particular combines attention to breath with a harmonious and relaxing physical exercise which aims to promote a feeling of peace and wellbeing. As with all stress-related conditions, it is important to realise that you are not alone and that there are people who are willing and able to help you.

Aromatic Solutions

Essential oils which are calming, reduce anxiety and prevent panic attacks are the ones to help in cases of hyperventilation. Clary sage, frankincense, jasmine, lavender, marjoram, melissa, neroli, orange, rose and ylang-ylang are all calming oils which can be used to counteract hysteria, palpitations and hyperventilation. Any one or two (in dilution) may be massaged into the hands, feet or neck of someone who is becoming distraught and in danger of hyperventilating. Whilst massaging, talk firmly and calmly and encourage the person to breathe out fully so that there is no breath left in the lungs. This may be enough to start them breathing normally again; when they do take in a large breath, they will be taking in aromas which will calm and soothe them.

Massage Blends for Hyperventilation

10 ml sweet almond *or* equivalent base oil
2 drops orange
1 drop marjoram
1 drop clary sage
    or
10 ml sweet almond
1 drop lavender
2 drops neroli
    or
10 ml sweet almond
1 drop ylang-ylang
2 drops lavender

A useful first aid measure to prevent hyperventilation is to open a bottle of peppermint or basil and take a deep breath. So if you have a friend or partner who is under a lot of stress and appears to be on the edge, it is advisable to carry around a small bottle of one of these oils. A little like a Victorian lady's smelling salts, these essential oils have very powerful aromas which sharpen the mind, increase the ability to concentrate on the task in hand, and have a grounding effect.

Regular aromatic baths are also helpful for anyone who regularly hyperventilates. Use the oils listed above to induce calm, rhythmic breathing and relaxation.

Other Alternatives

Acupuncture, Bach flower remedies, cranio-sacral therapy, homeopathy, hypnotherapy, shiatsu.

Immune Deficiency

Our immune system constitutes our defence against invasion from micro-organisms. White cells circulating in our blood arrest any foreign body and take it to one of the lymph nodes where an antibody is produced. Specially constructed to attach to the protein coat of the particular invader (known as the antigen), the antibodies seek out the organism and render it harmless. Each particular type of antibody is kept in store in case the threat returns.

Keeping our immune system strong and healthy is clearly a wise move. A deficient immune system is now being implicated in an ever-widening group of illnesses ranging from rheumatoid arthritis to cancer and, most obviously, to AIDS. The importance of a healthy diet with good levels of vitamins and minerals, satisfying sleep and exercise are important for health, and it is becoming increasingly clear that stress depresses the immune system and makes illness more likely. Someone who has been free of colds and flu for years on end can, after a period of emotional, financial or other stress, suddenly become ill. Germs have always been around, but the body has been able to resist them; then suddenly the defences are down and those germs can gain a foothold.

General Guidelines

Good, refreshing sleep is vital. It is while the body is asleep that the immune system can repair itself in pre-paration for the day ahead.

Diet
Eat good food when you are hungry, but avoid over- or under-eating. Going on crash diets can seriously under-mine the proper functioning of the immune system. Our pursuit of the perfect figure could result in a terrible illness, which is too high a price to pay.

Think positive
Always think positive thoughts rather than negative ones. Recent research, notably in the United States, has proved the existence of a link between our state of health and our state of mind. It is known as psycho-neuro-immunology or PNI. Our mind and emotions transmit messages through our nervous system which have an effect on our immune system. The nature of that effect depends on whether the thoughts are positive or nega-tive.

Talk
Seeking help for problems is not being a wimp. We shouldn't try to carry the weight of the world on our shoulders, but so often that is what we attempt to do. The resultant weight of emotions, phobias and despair can

rob us of our health by shutting down the very process we
need in order to stay healthy – the immune system.

Drugs and alcohol
Avoid substances that negatively affect the immune
system. Recreational drugs, and many prescribed drugs
such as antibiotics, have negative effects. So too can
alcohol, and there is a fine line between the amount of
alcohol that the body can handle, and the amount that is
too much for comfort.

Sex
Too many sexual partners can reduce the immune response simply because semen can prove to be an allergen.
When two people have sexual intercourse on a regular
basis, the body learns to accept the semen and it does not
cause a problem. However, when a person has numerous
sexual partners semen is never fully accepted by the body,
which treats it in the same way as a bacteria or virus – by
producing antibodies. So large numbers of sexual partners can have the same effect on the body as a bout of flu –
a lowering of the immune system.

The combined effect
If sexual promiscuity is accompanied by poor nutrition
(such as living on junk foods), negative thought patterns,
the regular use of recreational drugs or alcohol and insuffi-
cent sleep, the body's defences will deteriorate progessively
until that person catches everything that is going. In other
words, the person has acquired, by his or her own behaviour,
a deficiency of the immune system. If it is possible to acquire
deficiency of the immune system, it is equally possible to
acquire sufficiency of the immune system.

Aromatic Solutions

Bathing in aromatic water is one of the easiest ways to
stay in peak health. Essential oils not only scent the skin

but work their way through the body, imparting health and wellbeing (see Chapter 3). To build up the immune system there are dozens of suitable essential oils to choose from, but I have a small list of tried and tested ones which I feel are particularly useful. They are bergamot, lavender, ravansara, sandalwood and tea tree. Tea tree on its own does not smell very appealing and should be used in combination with one of the others. Add 2–3 drops of each chosen oil to a full bath of water, swish the water around thoroughly and soak for half an hour. Have this strengthening bath at least twice a week.

Massage
The same oils as above may be used in massage, and there are many combinations from which to choose what suits your sense of smell. Experiment to find a fragrance that you really like and want to use again and again, as you would an expensive perfume. But this particular 'perfume' could be your best investment ever in terms of health and resilience to disease.

Massage Blends for Immune Deficiency
15ml sweet almond 2 drops ravansara 2 drops lavender 1 drop tea tree *or* 15ml sweet almond 3 drops sandalwood 2 drops bergamot 1 drop thyme-linalol *or* 15ml sweet almond 2 drops sandalwood 1 drop lavender 3 drops bergamot

Room fragrancing
This is an easy way to incorporate the use of essential oils into your daily life. A few drops of any of the listed oils above can be added to the receptacle of a candle fragrancer, or to a bowl of hot water. Other essential oils with which to fragrance your home or work environment include frankincense, geranium, lemon, myrtle, orange and rosemary.

All essential oils are antiseptic to one degree or another, so any oil you choose for fragrancing will be helpful. If you have trouble sleeping, see INSOMNIA; if you are depressed or anxious, see DEPRESSION or ANXIETY.

Treatment of minor health matters
There are many ailments which can be treated with essential oils, which, if used at the start of the illness or disease, are often all that is needed to cure something which would otherwise have to be treated with antibiotics. Antibiotics are destructive to the immune system and should only be used as a last resort. Essential oils can be used in gargles to cure a sore throat (see COLDS AND FLU); in douches to clear up CANDIDA ALBICANS; and in compresses to treat digestive problems (see CONSTIPATION and INDIGESTION), to name but a few. There is not room in this book to go into specific detail, and I would recommend readers, whatever their gender, to refer to my book *Aromatherapy for Women*.

Other Alternatives

Acupuncture, Bach flower remedies, homeopathy, McTimony chiropractic, NLP, vitamin therapy.

Indigestion

Also known as dyspepsia, indigestion makes itself known by a sensation of pain or discomfort in the upper abdomen or lower chest. Possible accompanying symptoms are flatulence and nausea. Treatment aims to tackle the underlying cause, and if there is no evidence of an organic problem such as ulcers the reason is usually either what the sufferer has eaten or stress.

The solar plexus is the network of nerves situated behind the stomach which supply the abdominal organs. In ancient times it was considered to be the seat of our deeper feelings: the belief that our emotions can affect our digestion has a long history. Most of us have suffered at one time or another from nervous indigestion, when, in response to stress, the stomach increases its production of acid. If the stomach is subjected to a surfeit of acid, as in habitual nervous indigestion, ulcers can develop, so it is wise to think of preventive medicine and to tackle the initial symptoms of indigestion and the underlying stress before more serious problems are allowed to occur.

General Guidelines

If you tend to get indigestion frequently it is important to think before you eat. Too many of us eat on the run – don't make time or space in our lives for a proper meal but grab a sandwich and eat it in the car, or when we're too busy to pay attention to the actual process of eating. Gulping down improperly chewed food is asking for trouble. We need to get into the habit of taking small but adequate meals that are consumed at an unhurried pace and consist of foods that don't aggravate our stomachs. Too much fat, spicy food and caffeine and too few vegetables and wholegrains, upset our digestive systems. Combine this with worry over an approaching business meeting or coping with the demands of a difficult toddler, and the pain of indigestion can really hit home.

Nevertheless, controlling the diet alone may not be enough to keep indigestion at bay. Emotional factors may also need to be addressed.

Indigestion is often blamed on excess stomach acid, as a result of which the sufferer takes an antacid tablet. However, indigestion can just as easily be caused by too little stomach acid, in which case an antacid tablet would be quite inappropriate (see Chapter 4).

Aromatic Solutions

As with nausea and sick headaches, peppermint oil has a very high success rate. When indigestion occurs after a hastily eaten meal or one eaten too close to bedtime, a drop of peppermint oil mixed well into in a little honey water will quickly relax the abdominal muscles and allow the stomach contents to settle.

Peppermint Drink
1 drop peppermint oil ½ teaspoon runny honey ½ cup warm water

Slowly sip half of the liquid whilst sitting up, and then lie down. If the indigestion persists, drink the rest of the peppermint water. This remedy can often cure indigestion in a matter of minutes.

Solar plexus massage
The application of a little lavender, rose or geranium oil to the solar plexus, followed by gentle pressure, is a guaranteed way to release tension from the abdomen and so ease away the discomfort of indigestion (see p. 109 for technique). A tiny amount of essential oil (as above) may be applied to the finger and then directly to

the solar plexus point, but it is preferable to mix up a massage blend to ensure that skin irritation does not occur.

Solar Plexus Massage Blends

1 teaspoon sweet almond
1 drop rose
    or
1 teaspoon sweet almond
1 drop lavender or geranium

Regular warm aromatic baths will help to relax a tense body, as well as to relax a tense mind. Tension in any form will interfere with the normal process of digestion.

Essences for a Relaxing Bath

Bergamot
Clarysage
Frankincense
Geranium
Lavender
Lemon
Melissa
Neroli
Rose
Rosewood
Verbena
Ylang-ylang

Add 6–8 drops of any one of these to a full bath of warm water.

Other Alternatives

Acupuncture, homeopathy, reflexology.
    See also NAUSEA AND VOMITING.

Insomnia

Sleep means more than just rest. It is a time when the whole body can recuperate from the activities of the previous day, renewing cells and energy levels so that you will wake refreshed and ready to deal with another new day.

At one time or another nearly all of us will encounter some sleep problem. It can vary from the occasional nightmare to recurrent insomnia, and if the disturbance continues then the normal processes of daily life become affected. There are many causes of sleeplessness, ranging from a new baby to a snoring partner. Distressing though they may be, these kinds of situation can be remedied by the baby being pacified or the partner being turned on to his side. What we know as insomnia, however, is a different kind of sleeplessness. It occurs when there is no external reason why the person concerned is awake. The room may be quiet and dark and the bed warm and comfortable – it is the 'noise' going on inside our own mind that is keeping us awake. Worry and stress are high on the list for most insomniacs as they mull over the events of the day or conversations that have upset them.

When this scenario is repeated night after night the sufferer may resort to asking a GP for sleeping tablets. But this type of medication, although beneficial in the short term at times of bereavement or similar cases of severe trauma, is in general ill advised. Sleeping pills fail to tackle the underlying cause, and can in themselves lead to further problems. One in three people suffers from insomnia, with thousands of prescriptions for tablets being written every day.

General Guidelines

For those who find getting to sleep a problem, setting the mood will almost certainly help. Spending the evening doing something relaxing or taking exercise will prepare the body and mind for what is to come. An evening spent dealing with problems or mountains of paperwork, on the other hand, or rehashing old worries, will only leave the mind over-active as bedtime approaches. Avoid stimulants such as cigarettes or caffeine-based drinks in the evening. A hot milky drink, sipped slowly in a warm bed with some gentle music playing, will assist you in your aim of getting some peaceful, restful sleep.

Some people wake very early in the morning and find it difficult to go back to sleep. Rather than lying in the dark trying hard to feel sleepy again, it is often better not to try. A good book to delve into or some favourite music to listen to may be all it takes to remind your body and mind that you are in fact still tired.

Aromatic Solutions

There are several sedative oils which, if used before bedtime, will help to relax both body and mind ready for a peaceful night. Probably the most popular of all sedative essential oils is lavender, which is most commonly used as a lavender bath. Run a bath of comfortably warm water and add ten drops of lavender oil.

Make sure that you are buying a pure lavender oil, which has a very low concentration of camphor – certainly not enough to interfere with sleep. Spike lavender, however, has a high concentration of camphor which, since it is stimulating, will awaken rather than sedate and should not be used at night. A lavandin is a cross between pure lavender and spike lavender and will contain varying amounts of camphor.

Insomnia is very debilitating and, when experienced over a long period, can have serious effects on your health. Regular back massages, either from a professional masseuse or from a friend, will encourage your body to relax and let go of stored tension, choose from: linden blossom, melissa, vetivert, camomile, marjoram, lavender, neroli, rose or geranium.

Relaxing Massage Oil
15ml sweet almond *or* equivalent base oil 3 drops lavender 1 drop geranium 1 drop rose *or* neroli (optional) 2 drops marjoram

Other Alternatives

Acupuncture, Bach flower remedies, cranio-sacral therapy, Homeopathy, hypnotherapy, McTimony chiropractic, NLP, psychotherapy, reflexology.

Irritable Bowel Syndrome (IBS)

The exact cause of irritable bowel syndrome is unclear, but most sufferers can pinpoint its beginnings to an acute attack of gastro-enteritis, a course of antibiotics, an abdominal operation or a stressful period in their lives. The condition has a collection of symptoms: abdominal pain, constipation alternating with diarrhoea, bloated abdomen and the passing of mucus with stools or by itself.

IBS is not life-threatening and does not precede ulcerative colitis or cancer, but sufferers often worry that it is a sign of more serious illness. This anxiety in itself can often worsen the condition, so it is wise to seek reassurance from your doctor.

The condition in itself can cause severe stress as sufferers worry about such practical considerations as the availability of toilets, the food they may be offered in a friend's home or restaurant, and the noise that their stomach might make. Thus anxiety about the effects of IBS exacerbates the condition itself, and the person becomes trapped in a vicious circle.

General Guidelines

A number of books have been written which give advice on all aspects of IBS, diet and stress being the two main fronts on which to tackle the problem. Following a diet formulated with the help of your doctor or dietitian, will help to isolate foods that cause trouble. Many sufferers have found that paying attention to what they eat makes an enormous difference and which may completely alleviate the discomfort. Certain foods can, by their very nature, stimulate excessive muscle contractions in the bowel wall of susceptible people.

People often worry about the inconvenience it causes others if they are avoiding particular foods, so it might be advisable to take a rain check on dinner invitations and so on and make getting to the root of the problem your first priority. Taking care of the stressful factors in your life and feeling in control will ultimately have a beneficial effect on all your body systems, including your digestive system.

Aromatic Solutions

Peppermint oil is the remedy *par excellence* for the treatment of irritable bowel syndrome. It is simultaneously anti-inflammatory, slightly analgesic, antibacterial and calming. The oil can be administered in a number of ways. It may be taken orally – pure peppermint oil is what flavours our after-dinner mints as well as our toothpastes and mouthwashes. Taking the peppermint drink on p. 212 once or twice a day should be enough to make the soothing benefits of this oil noticeable. Alternatively, try a compress.

Abdominal compress
Pour one drop of peppermint or camomile oil into a small bottle of water and shake well. Add this to a bowl of warm

water. Dip a small towel into the peppermint water, wring
it out and apply to the abdomen. Lie still for fifteen
minutes or so, if necessary covering the compress with
a blanket or large dry towel. (see p. 115 for technique).
Take with either 6 drops geranium or lavender.

Other Alternatives

Acupuncture, applied kinesiology, Cranio-sacral therapy,
homeopathy, hynotherapy, NLP, vitamin therapy.

Joint Pains

A joint is the meeting-place between different parts of the
skeleton, whether bones or cartilage. Spasm of the muscles around the joint, often due to stress and tension,
leads to pain and stiffness in the joint itself. This can lead
to inflammation and thickening of the lining of the
capsule in which the joint is contained.

Joint pain is debilitating and often restricts the life of
the sufferer. And, as is so often the case with stress
reactions, a vicious circle can be set up as the sufferer
worries about encroaching disability and finds that the
more he or she worries, the worse the condition becomes.

Arthritis is the name commonly given to joint pains,
whether of an acute or chronic nature. There are two
types of arthritis: inflammatory, which includes acute
poly-arthritis and rheumatoid arthritis; and degenerative
or osteo-arthritis. Acute poly-arthritis, that which affects
a number of joints, can be a frightening experience, as it
is so sudden. Joints which yesterday seemed normal are
today too painful to use. This condition normally corrects
itself within a few weeks, but does require adequate bed
rest so that the condition does not deteriorate into anything permanent. Stress may be the precipitating cause.

General Guidelines

Prescribed painkillers and anti-inflammatory drugs may relieve joint pain but do not tackle the root cause. Many sufferers are now turning to more holistic treatments that aim to return the joint to a more natural function. Diet, hydrotherapy and acupuncture, to name but a few, have a proven track record with such conditions. Drink plenty of pure water but avoid carbonated mineral water, as carbon-dioxide makes the blood too alkaline, and this will ultimately cause more pain to the joints.

It is important to protect your joints and to avoid any kind of physical exercise that may cause the pain to worsen. Cold, damp weather is often a problem, so keeping warm and dry needs to be a priority. Being overweight adds extra strain to all the body systems, but joints such as knees and hips are expected to bear much of the extra load. There are many books that explain diets which will not only help you regain your ideal weight but also cut out foods known to aggravate joint pains.

Aromatic Solutions

Inflammatory arthritis can be considerably improved with essential oils, especially those such as camomile, lavender and juniper which have anti-inflammatory properties. Osteo-arthritis cannot be cured with aromatherapy; however the pain can be substantially lessened, and a greater mobility is found in the joints of the knees, hips and hands when aromatic oils are regularly employed. Of particular help are black pepper, camomile, lavender, marjoram and rosemary.

Anti-inflammatory Oil for Massage in Arthritis
15 ml jojoba 2 drops camomile 2 drops lavender

Arthritis Blend to Decrease Pain and Increase Mobility
15 ml jojoba 1 drop black pepper 2 drops juniper 2 drops rosemary 2 drops lavender

If the joint pain is not too severe to allow you to climb into a bath, a regular soak in a comfortably hot lavender bath will help relax your entire body, including muscles that have tensed during the day as a response to pain. If you don't like lavender, any essential oil which helps you to relax and feel positive about your body will be of benefit. Choose from bergamot, palmarosa, clary sage, frankincense, geranium, juniper, myrtle, rosemary and ylang-ylang.

Other Alternatives

Acupuncture, applied Kiniesiology, cranio-sacral therapy, McTimony chiropractic, NLP, reflexology, shiatsu.

ME

See POST VIRAL SYNDROME

Menstruation

See AMENORRHOEA, DYSMENORRHOEA

Migraine

See HEADACHES AND MIGRAINE

Nausea and Vomiting

To feel nauseous is to experience an uncomfortable feeling in your stomach which suggests that you are about to vomit. It can range from butterflies in the stomach – which we have all experienced before such events as an interview, boarding an aircraft, going to a party and meeting someone for the first time – to more severe and debilitating attacks in which the sufferer feels very unwell and has to lie down. Many forms of nausea have a physiological cause, such as during pregnancy when the hormone balance is altered, or when taking prescription drugs. Nausea may also be a result of seeing or smelling something which revolts us and is the body's natural reaction – an attempt to get rid of the image or aroma.

Stress-induced nausea usually accompanies anxiety or acute nervousness. Problems at work or with family members can be a major cause, as can bereavement or financial problems. In many cases the person will get up in the morning and feel unable to face breakfast. Undoubtedly it is the anticipation of the trouble ahead that upsets their normal appetite. The feeling usually fades during the day, but for some people the problem can become severe enough to cause dizziness and vomiting.

General guidelines

If possible, talk about your worries, fears or hurts to someone in whom you can confide. The old cliché that a problem shared is a problem halved still holds true, and there are facilities to speak to a counsellor or psychotherapist in every major town. Not everyone feels comfortable about expressing their innermost feelings to another person, however, and if this is true of you then commit your thoughts to paper. Get it off your chest by writing down your feelings, your problems, your aspirations. Perhaps you will want to write a letter expressing your hurt.

When vomiting is occurring on more than just the odd occasion, and you have ruled out pregnancy, food poisoning or a tummy bug, it is a sure sign that the adrenal glands have become completely exhausted. In this instance it is of prime importance to get the adrenals functioning properly before attempting to deal with any emotional or physical problems which may be causing stress. The safest and fastest way to do so is by taking a large (5–10g) dose of vitamin C in the form of magnesium ascorbate each morning. Visit a nutritionist who can advise on the best foods to eat.

Aromatic Solutions

The aromatic essence to reach for first in cases of nausea is oil of peppermint. The high menthol content in pure peppermint oil (*Mentha piperata*) enables it to register instantly in the brain, calming and soothing the vagus nerve which runs from the brain to the stomach. It is also, surprisingly, both warming and cooling. If taken internally (see p. 212 for recipe) it induces a warm, comforting feeling in the stomach which instantly relaxes taut stomach muscles and takes away the tension and fear of vomiting which often accompany nausea. Sip one teaspoon every five minutes until the nausea subsides.

If pure oil is not available, or you are uncertain of the quality of your oil, an alternative remedy is to make a small cup of peppermint tea (herbal teas are nowadays available in supermarkets as well as health food stores). The addition of a little honey will hasten the process by which the peppermint enters the bloodstream. Very often a single cup of either peppermint drink or peppermint tea will relieve nausea.

Peppermint oil may also be used externally as a compress. Another oil which has a remarkable success rate at easing nausea is Roman camomile, which is also easily applied in the form of a compress. Place a face flannel, handkerchief or small towel into the solution below, wring out the excess liquid, place the compress over the stomach and lie down for fifteen to thirty minutes. Peppermint oil feels cool to the skin, so when using this oil cover the wet compress with a large dry towel to avoid feeling chilly.

Abdominal Compress for Nausea

1–2 drops peppermint *or* camomile added to 250–500 ml bottle of water. Shake very thoroughly and add to ½ litre hottish water

---

Other Alternatives

Acupuncture, Bach flower remedies, homeopathy, hypnotherapy, NLP, vitamin therapy.

Neck Pain

The neck is the passageway between the head and the body and at its centre are seven cervical vertebrae which are held by muscles attached in front and behind. Since muscular contraction is one of the body's first reactions to stress, it is not surprising that neck pain is one of the most common indications of encroaching tension. The muscles of the neck contract, and gradually the tension spreads up the back of the head and/or down towards the shoulders. Continuous neck tension results in muscle fibre becoming bunched up so that it feels as though there are rocks under the skin. If allowed to remain, the result will be loss of mobility of the neck, pain on movement, and irritability. The discomfort intereferes with the ability to work, sleep properly or enjoy leisure activities.

Common physical causes of neck pain include driving for long periods or stop-start in a traffic jam, and lifting or carrying heavy objects.

General Guidelines

It is very easy to develop bad posture if you feel cold, so it is important to keep your neck warm so that you do not hunch up your shoulders. Try at all times to hold your head erect, and if necessary take Alexander Technique lessons which will directly align your neck and spine. The average adult head weighs approximately 4 kilos, and if you spend long hours with your head bent over a desk the entire weight of your head is being held by the muscles at the back of your neck.

Another common reason for neck pain is sleeping in a bad position. A cylindrical neck pillow (a mini-bolster) will keep your neck in a slightly stretched position, which lessens strain on it during the night.

If you are stuck in a traffic jam, rotate your head by placing your left ear over your left shoulder, tilting your head back and then gently and slowly rotating your head to your right shoulder. Repeat from right to left. Never rotate your head more than 180 degrees, as turning the head full circle can actually create neck pain by putting too much strain on the neck muscles.

Aromatic Solutions

Massaging the neck releases tension and unlocks knotted muscles. A neck massage is easy to do, whether for yourself or your partner, and can be performed whilst sitting up or when lying down. Pile the hair on top of the head to get it out of the way, and apply a liberal amount of massage oil to your hands (see pages 104 and 111 for technique).

Neck Massage Oil
10ml sweet almond *or* other good-quality oil 1 drop sandalwood 1 drop bergamot 1 drop lavender *or* 10ml sweet almond 1 drop marjoram 1 drop rosemary 1 drop lavender

Take regular aromatic night-time baths to relax the shoulder muscles, which link with the neck muscles. The water temperature should be at body heat or just slightly higher, and the water deep enough to enable you to immerse yourself up to your chin. A small folded towel placed on the end of the bath will protect and cushion your neck whilst you lie back and relax. To a full bath add six drops of geranium, lavender, myrtle or ylang-ylang.

Anyone with severe or persistent neck pain would be advised to visit a professional aromatherapist or masseuse on a regular basis. If the pain continues even after the massage sessions, it is possible that you have a subluxation of the neck and should seek help from a McTimony chiropractor. Finally, create a tranquil home environment by vaporising relaxing oils of bergamot, lavender, myrtle, rose or rosewood in your living area and bedroom.

Other Alternatives

Cranio-sacral therapy, McTimothy chiropratic, reflexology, shiatsu.

See also SHOULDER PAIN.

Nose Bleeds

It is in the mucous membrane which lines the nose that
nose bleeds originate. Usually only one side is affected,
and in most cases the bleeding is easily stopped and only
a small amount of blood is lost. They are common in
childhood and often occur because of fragile blood vessels, after a blow to the nose, or sometimes in cases of
high blood pressure (see HYPERTENSION).

Severe stress without any apparent solution can,
especially in a young child, result in occasional nose
bleeds. It is a cry for help from the body itself, whilst
simultaneously releasing some of the mental pressure
which has built up. My eldest daughter suffered from
fairly regular and heavy nose bleeds during her first
two years of secondary education in a large school in
which she felt she never quite belonged. After we
moved her to a smaller school which was sympathetic
to vegetarianism and alternative medicine and was also
very art-orientated, my daughter's nose bleeds ceased
completely.

General Guidelines

Encourage your child to talk to you about any troubling matters. Let him or her know that you are
supportive and want to help, but won't interfere if
that is what he wants. Often children are reluctant
to discuss problems with their parents because doing
so makes other children despise them. On a practical
level it is important for the parent to keep calm, since
fear and panic often accompany the sight of blood.
Talk calmly and reassure your child that it looks
worse than it is, and that you will soon stop the
bleeding.

Aromatic Solutions

Lavender oil has many remarkable properties. It is very gentle on the skin and does not irritate the mucous membranes, which makes it ideal for dealing with a nose bleed. Another useful property is its styptic nature. Lavender's ability to halt the flow of blood within minutes of being applied to a fresh wound is remarkable. Put a drop or two of pure lavender oil on to the corner of a tissue or a small piece of cotton wool, and insert this into the affected nostril. Leave it in place for a few minutes, then check to see if the bleeding has stopped. Repeat the procedure until bleeding ceases.

In addition, a short massage of the shoulders and neck will go a long way towards releasing tension and assuring your child of your love and support. Choose essential oils that relax and pacify, such as geranium, vetivert, neroli, rose, clary sage or marjoram.

Massage Blends for Nose Bleed
10 ml sweet almond or other fatty oil
1 drop geranium
1 drop marjoram
1 drop lavender
or
10 ml sweet almond
1 drop vetivert
1 drop rose
1 drop lavender

There are two things to avoid in cases of nose bleed. Do not blow your nose, as this can start the bleeding off again. Also do not lie flat on your back, which causes blood to seep backwards into the throat, giving rise to further distress.

Other alternatives

Applied kinesiology, cranio-sacral therapy, homeopathy.

Pain

See BACK PAIN, JOINT PAINS, NECK PAIN, SHOULDER PAIN.

Post Viral Syndrome

This condition, also known as ME and chronic fatigue syndrome, causes profound mental and physical fatigue. Considered to be viral in origin, it usually follows infections such as glandular fever or hepatitis but can also be the result of prolonged or acute stress, when it is thought that a dormant virus takes advantage of the weakened immune system (see IMMUNE DEFICIENCY).

The effect on the sufferer's life can be devastating, for despite an appearance of good health he or she will be unable to cope with the basic effort involved in daily living. The disease itself becomes a new stress as the sufferer is no longer able to work, care for her children or tackle the multitude of tasks that we all generally deal with on a daily basis.

General Guidelines

It is important for you and those around you to accept that you are unwell and need to spend time resting and building up your immune system. Vitamin and mineral supplements are advisable to take, and a visit to a nutritionist would be extremely beneficial in pinpointing exactly which supplements to take and whether any foods should be excluded from the diet.

Many sufferers of post viral syndrome have led busy lives and find it difficult to adjust to a life of inactivity. However, the way back to health involves letting go of daily expectations and putting the little energy you do have into ensuring that you eat a healthy diet and get adequate rest. As your energy levels improve, the time will come to introduce gentle exercise to strengthen and revive yourself. The trick is not to do so much that it precipitates a relapse. Listening to your body's rhythms and acting accordingly is the way to success.

Aromatic Solutions

The most important essential oils to use for the treatment of post-viral syndrome are those which possess antiviral properties. Those commonly prescribed include tea tree, lavender and naiouli, but if I had to choose only one it would be ravansara. This fast-acting oil has a pleasant, unusual aroma like a mild blend of eucalyptus and cloves.

Massage Blends for Post Viral Syndrome
10ml sweet almond *or* equivalent base oil 3 drops ravansara 1 drop bergamot *or* lemon   *or* 10ml sweet almond 1 drop tea tree or thyme-linalol 2 drops lavender

Having post viral syndrome usually means that a virus has entered the body and, instead of being destroyed by the immune system, has taken up residence somewhere — it could be in the feet, it could be in the calves, it could be almost anywhere. If, for example, your calf muscles are constantly aching, that is where the virus is probably lying dormant. Massage affected parts of the body with the aromatic blend.

Take regular aromatic baths using any of the above listed oils. They will all help to improve the efficacy of your immune system.

People with post viral syndrome often have difficulty in getting to sleep at night, and may also suffer from depression. If this applies to you, see INSOMNIA and DEPRESSION.

Other Alternatives

Acupuncture, applied kinesiology, Bach flower remedies, cranio-sacral therapy, homeopathy, NLP, reflexology, vitamin therapy.

Psoriasis

This common skin disease affects about 2 per cent of the population and tends to be genetic. It is characterised by thickened patches of inflamed, red skin, often covered by silvery scales, and the affected area may be in patches around the knees and elbows or may extend to cover large parts of the torso. These skin eruptions are sometimes accompanied by painful swelling and stiffness of the joints, which can further disable and embarrass the sufferer.

The disease can vary in severity, triggered by factors such as skin damage, physical illness or emotional stress. Although the psoriasis itself may not originate from emotional upset, there is no doubt that stress can worsen the condition or indeed bring on an attack. For example, just before examinations the skin of a sufferer will suddenly break out badly.

General Guidelines

Many sufferers of psoriasis are prescribed cortico-steroid creams which work by suppressing inflammation — our body's reaction to infection. By blocking this process we deny the body its ability to heal in the normal way, and it is for this reason that such creams should be used with caution.

Living with psoriasis means taking care of your skin. Regular bathing with simple soap which does not aggravate the skin is advisable. Some doctors recommend preparations with coal tar, but this acts in a similar way to steroids and is best avoided. Since the affected patches may bleed after only minor injuries, do protect your hands with gloves when working in the house and garden. The skin is also less liable to crack if kept supple with emulsifying ointments.

Staying positive and confident in yourself is important, because such a visible skin problem can affect your body image. Talking over any worries or fears and making sure you get adequate rest can also help to prevent it getting worse. Recent research has proved the importance of sleep in recharging our immune system, which plays a vital role in enhancing and maintaining the health of all the body systems.

Aromatic Solutions

As psoriasis is very closely associated with stress it is wise to take regular aromatic baths with those essential oils which promote relaxation and enhance the working of the immune system. They include bergamot, camomile, geranium, lavender, rose, palmarosa and sandalwood. Include a few drops of at least one of these in a full bath of water, and take at least one aromatic bath a week.

Psoriasis feels worse if the surrounding skin is allowed to become too dry, so make yourself a simple massage oil and apply a little each day. People with psoriasis should use essential oils only in very dilute amounts.

Massage Blend for Psoriasis
20 ml sweet almond 2 drops lavender 1 drop camomile 1 drop bergamot *or* 20 ml sweet almond 3 drops sandalwood 1 drop geranium

Other Alternatives

Acupuncture, cranio-sacral therapy, homeopathy, NLP, reflexology, vitamin therapy.

Recovery from Heart Attack

Myocardial infarction, in which an area of heart muscle is denied oxygen, is the single most common cause of death in developed countries. Characterised by severe, unremitting chest pain, breathlessness and cold, clammy skin, a heart attack is experienced by a quarter of a million people in Britain each year. More than half of these people die, while the others go on to rebuild their lives.

The risk factors for heart attack are well documented and include high blood pressure (see HYPERTENSION) smoking, high-fat diet, obesity, overworking and severe stress. Recovery involves tackling the same risk factors if another heart attack is to be avoided.

Some stress is a necessary component in all our lives, but when stress levels are high a feeling of hopelessness and loss of control soon follows. At the end of the day we feel dissatisfied and go to bed with our head full of problems. Chronic stress sets in and before long our body is coping with a habitually racing pulse, INDIGESTION, high blood pressure and other associated symptoms. Clearly a person recovering from heart attack needs to manage their stress levels in order not to strain an already compromised heart. Learning to relax and let go, mentally and physically, is an important part of this process.

General Guidelines

All of us at some point allow our standards to slide – a few pounds gained each year, two glasses of wine in the evening instead of one, too much going on at work or at home for the exercise we once enjoyed. It's a familiar picture, repeated all over the Western world. However, at some time our bodies will force us to slow down and give our wellbeing priority. Recovering from a heart attack takes time, and it is important to have an understanding of the factors that may have precipitated the illness and thus avoid history repeating itself. A healthy heart is dependent on the materials we feed it and the load we expect it to bear. The risk factors listed above need to be considered and a personal plan worked out, taking into account:

- *Diet:* which should be low in fats, refined sugars and salt, and high in vitamins and minerals, fresh vegetables and fruit.
- *Smoking:* give up or at least cut down.
- *Alcohol:* give up or at least cut down.
- *Exercise:* together with a healthy diet, exercise is the next most popular form of preventive medicine. It will help people to come to terms with their own bodies and

to deal with any weight problem. This in turn will ease
hypertension, build and strengthen muscle and increase stamina.

● *Take time out to slow down and relax.* Accept certain
limitations, and deal with the stresses of everyday life
so that there is no compromise of life itself.

Aromatic Solutions

Since stress plays such a big part in the onset of heart
disease, in order to prevent a second attack it is important to de-stress the body and learn to live life at a
sensible pace. Many essential oils are ideal for de-stressing; the ones most pertinent to recovery from heart
attack are geranium, marjoram, melissa, neroli, palmarosa, rosemary, sandalwood and ylang-ylang.

Neroli is being used to great effect in intensive
therapy units throughout Britain. This oil reduces
tension and allays anxiety, two common companions
to survivors of a heart attack. Neroli can be massaged
into the shoulders, the feet or the hands – whatever is
convenient to reach. Very often a heart attack victim
will be attached to lots of hi-tech equipment, which
looks very daunting both to the patient and to visitors.
Just explain your intentions to the nurse in charge of
the ITU, and you should be able to massage the hands
or feet with ease. It may, however, not be possible to
massage the shoulders until the patient is well enough
to sit up unaided.

Once the patient is allowed home it is beneficial to take
regular aromatic baths using six to ten drops of any one
of the oils listed above. Just add the essence to a full bath
of warm water and swish the water thoroughly.

Room Fragrancing
Inhale peaceful and calming aromas by putting a drop or
two of an essential oil in a bowl of warm water or in the
water receptacle of a candle fragrancer. Choose from

geranium, lavender, melissa, neroli, palmarosa, rose or ylang-ylang.

Other Alternatives

Bach flower remedies, cranio-sacral therapy, homeopathy, NLP, reflexology, vitamin therapy.

Sexual Problems

Problems to do with sex fall into two categories: physical and psychological. Physical reasons for inhibited desire or inability to achieve erection include disorders of the endocrine system, prolonged alcohol abuse, some drug therapies (including antihistamines for the treatment of hay fever) and tenderness after childbirth.

Psychological reasons, however, are far more common, as the way we view ourselves can powerfully affect our body's response. As is often the case with stress, one symptom leads to another and what begins as a simple case of tiredness can lead to anxiety and a feeling of hopelessness until our body image is distorted and our sexual confidence is affected. Making love becomes charged with tension and fear of failure, and it becomes impossible to let go and enjoy the moment.

General Guidelines

In order to enjoy our own sexuality we need to feel confident with our bodies and our ability to express ourselves. There is no doubt that when we take regular exercise and pay attention to our diet we feel the positive effects: our bodies become trimmer and lose that sluggish feeling that often goes with inactivity and poor eating habits. A good diet containing all the necessary vitamins and minerals, especially vitamin C and zinc, together with adequate rest, will often lift our energy levels and dispel the black cloud of despondency and sexual anxiety.

If fear of failure is a problem, this can be solved by talking openly with your partner or by just making sure you are relaxed enough beforehand to allow all your anxieties to recede into the background. A dose of courage can come in many forms, not least in the guise of essential oils which have the power to relax and heal.

Aromatic Solutions

An ideal combination of essential oils to use would be those oils that uplift mentally yet relax physically. Into this category come bergamot, clary sage, geranium, myrtle, rose, sandalwood, verbena and ylang-ylang. Any one of these may be used in baths (either singly or blended with other essential oils), in a massage blend, as a room fragrancer, or as a perfume. Other essential oils which relax and allay anxiety are lavender, lemon, neroli, orange, patchouli, rosewood, palmarosa and vetivert.

Aromatic baths for sexual problems
To a full bath of warm water add a maximum of 10 drops of essential oil from the above list. Agitate the water to ensure that the oils disperse before stepping into the bath.

Sample Bath Blend for Sexual Problems
2 drops geranium 6 drops myrtle 2 drops ylang-ylang

Massage
Sometimes it is advisable to make up massage blends in small quantities (10ml at a time), but in the case

of sexual problems which may require regular treatment over a long period it is preferable to make up a 100ml bottle of massage oil. This will be enough for ten to twenty massages, depending upon the area of the body massaged and how much oil is absorbed into your skin – some skins soak up oils, whilst others do not.

Massage Blends for Sexual Problems

100ml sweet almond *or* equivalent base oil
5–10 drops rose
10–20 drops sandalwood
5–10 drops bergamot
      or
100ml sweet almond
10 drops clary sage
10 drops sandalwood
10 drops myrtle
      or
100ml sweet almond
10 drops ylang-ylang
10 drops patchouli
10 drops orange

Any of the above blends can be used for a back massage, a solar plexus massage, a foot or hand massage, or a neck and shoulder massage (see p. 99 onwards for techniques).

Room Fragrancer
Any of the above essential oils may be used to fragrance the bedroom or living area of your home. To a bowl of hot water or a candle or electric fragrancer add one to five drops of your chosen oil. Once you have discovered which are your favourite essences you may like to use two or three together.

Other Alternatives

Acupuncture, cranio-sacral therapy, homeopathy, hypno-therapy, NLP, psychotherapy, reflexology, shiatsu.

Shingles

This is the popular name for herpes zoster, an infection of the nerves that supply certain areas of the skin. Caused by the varicella-zoster virus, which is also responsible for chickenpox, it is distinguished by a painful rash of small, crusting blisters which spread in zones around the waist and chest and may even encroach on to the face, particularly on the brow and around the eye. Following the attack, one-third of sufferers will experience pain from damaged nerves which can last for several months or even years.

The virus starts off in the body as chickenpox. After an attack of chickenpox most of the viral organisms will have been destroyed, but some may lie dormant in the body until the immune system is compromised (see IM-MUNE DEFICIENCY) and the virus is able to re-emerge. It is not unusual for shingles to follow a period of stress, and it is commonly seen in people with AIDS or cancer. Clearly, the health of our immune system is the vital link in preventing this illness.

General Guidelines

The quality of the food you eat is very important. Increase your intake of fresh fruit and vegetables, especially if your diet has tended towards fast foods and snacking through lack of time and pressures of work. It is vital to build up your immune system so that your body has reserves with which to tackle the virus which causes shingles. Plenty of rest is important because the immune system is replenished while we are asleep, and it is a big mistake to imagine that we can fight our way through a viral illness by sheer will-power. Good refreshing sleep is important, and so too is daytime cat-napping if you can find the time. Accept the fact that you have shingles, rather than being ashamed of it. Stress has allowed the condition to occur in your body in the first place; anxiety about the illness will not help it to go away and may make it worse.

Aromatic Solutions

Antiviral and soothing essential oils are best for treating shingles. Into these categories come the following.

Antiviral	Soothing
Eucalyptus	Bergamot
Lavender	Camomile
Niaouli	Geranium
Ravansara	Lavender
Tea tree	Linden blossom
	Melissa
	Rose

Choose one oil from each category and add three drops of each to a full bath of warm water. Soak every evening before going to bed. You will feel better in yourself, and your body will be in a receptive state for restful and healing sleep.

During the day, if you are plagued by incessant itching a peppermint compress is recommended. The menthol content will cool the skin and relieve the irritating itch which so often accompanies shingles.

Compress for Shingles
Add one drop of peppermint oil to a small bottle of water
and shake well. Then add this mixture to ½ litre warm
water. Dip a piece of material into the warm liquid to
make compress (see p. 115 for technique).

Other Alternatives

Bach flower remedies, cranio-sacral therapy, homeopathy,
reflexology, vitamin therapy.

Shoulder Pain

Stiffness or pain in the shoulder is often associated with
stress. Such aches and pains are sometimes called fibrositis, a vague term which indicates pain around muscles
and joints. Another popular name for this affliction is
frozen shoulder. The condition is produced by inflammation of the bursa that normally prevents friction between
the joint and the surrounding tissues. It can be caused by
trauma to the shoulder, for example trying to move a
large piece of furniture.
    Shoulder pain is also commonly related to posture and
to the working environment. There is no doubt that stress
leads to prolonged contraction of the shoulder muscles,
and many people are aware of their shoulders gradually
hunching with tension as the day goes by.

General Guidelines

Although not a serious condition, pain in this area can
cause extreme discomfort. Becoming aware of your body,
especially the shape of your back, is vital. Encouraging
your shoulders backwards and downwards leads to a

lengthening of the spine, allows the blood to flow as it is meant to, and helps prevent your back and shoulder muscles from going into spasm. Yoga is a marvellous way of relearning a relaxed and harmonious posture, and once the basic principles are clear they can be practised at work or at home or in potentially stressful situations. Alexander Technique is also useful. Common-sense measures such as avoiding draughts and being well wrapped up in cold weather are helpful, as is the avoidance of carrying heavy weights such as suitcases, over-full briefcases or shopping bags. Regular, controlled exercise to strengthen your back muscles and generally tone up the tissue is also worth considering.

Aromatic Solutions

The essential oils to choose should be those which have anti-inflammatory properties such as camomile, lavender, frankincense and tea tree.

Massage Oil for Shoulder Pain
10ml sweet almond or equivalent base oil 3 drops lavender + 2 drops myrtle   *or* 10ml sweet almond 3 drops tea tree

Massage the affected shoulder every day, applying generous amouts of oil. If possible, get your partner to apply the oil and gently massage the shoulder joint.

Other Alternatives

Applied kinesiology, cranio-sacral therapy, McTimony chiropractic, shiatsu.
See also NECK PAIN.

Stomach Ache

Many of us get vague abdominal pains when suffering from stress. It can range from a feeling of 'butterflies in the stomach' to more severe pain, when the stomach muscles feel contracted and knotted. Some of us may hold our problems within us, and unwittingly tense our abdomen until the pain drives us to use antacids or visit our doctor for advice.

When any organic causes have been ruled out, we need to look at our lifestyle, dietary habits, exercise patterns and stress levels. Keeping a diary that records when the pain comes and goes is often a good way of finding triggers. Certain stresses in life cannot be avoided, but perhaps our reaction to them can change. Once we have acquired insight into our own individual patterns, we can recognise the danger signs and develop mechanisms for coping.

General Guidelines

When you feel your stomach churn it is a common reaction to focus on the discomfort in an effort to make it go away. But often that sets up tension which causes the pain to worsen rather than ease. This unfortunate cycle can, however, be broken if you make the effort to relax and accept your body's reaction without judging ourselves. Turning your attention away from the pain through deep breathing, gentle music, a good book or closing your office door for twenty minutes' peace may be all it takes to restore equilibrium. Pay close attention to what you are eating, because something in your diet may be placing extra strain on an already sensitive part of your body. There will always be a time, however, when a nervous stomach is not so easy to deal with, and at such times it is helpful to turn to massage and essentials oils.

Aromatic Solutions

If the stomach ache has built up over the course of several hours and you know that the root cause has been your stressful day – rushing from task to task, eating on the trot, and feeling as though you have the weight of the world on your shoulders – then it is time to stop and allow your abdominal muscles to unlock and relax. Sometimes all you need is to take a soak in a comfortably hot bath. There are several relaxing essential oils to choose from, but the two most obvious choices would be lavender and geranium. To a full bath of water add up to eight drops of essential oil, either three of geranium and five of lavender or a combination to suit your smell preference. Mix the essences and water before you step in, and then lie back and relax. Relax for twenty to thirty minutes, and place a small pad or folded towel behind your neck for extra comfort. If you have a battery-operated cassette player take it into the bathroom and play a favourite piece of music so that your mind has something to concentrate on, allowing your body to let go of the stressful day which it has just experienced.

Massage Blend for Stomach Ache
10ml sweet almond *or* equivalent base oil 2 drops orange 1 drop geranium 1 drop lavender *or* 10ml sweet almond 1 drop peppermint 2 drops grapefruit

Sometimes tension can create a temporary blockage in the intestines when it seems as though food is just not passing through, but is stuck and causing acute discomfort. At times like this, a massage of the lower abdomen can be very helpful. The massage should be firm but not cause pain. Make up a massage blend and apply it to your right hand. Place your hand on your tummy and, working in a clockwise direction, sweep your hand around your navel so that the entire abdomen is covered. Do this slowly and rhythmically, and gradually apply firmer pressure until you feel that the stomach ache is lessening. Then cover yourself up and lie down for ten minutes.

Other Alternatives

Applied kinesiology, cranio-sacral therapy, homeopathy, reflexology, shiatsu.

Tension

When our minds become tense, so do our bodies. Time and external pressures can take over our lives until we feel driven by outside forces rather than in control of our own energy. Feelings become bottled up, and the strain associated with anxiety, anger or fear leads to a multitude of reactions within our bodies. Muscles are held in sustained contraction until we have aches and pains in various parts from stomach to jaw. Our breathing speeds up, as does our heart rate, and we begin to feel dizzy and nauseous. It isn't long before we feel drained of energy, perpetually tired and afraid that we can no longer cope with life.

General Guidelines

Feeling tense on a regular basis is a truly unpleasant experience, but there are tried and tested ways of alleviating such discomfort. Most importantly, we need to accept our limitations and be sure that others accept them too.

For most of us, the warning bells only start to sound when we are already overloaded. Pressures at work, at home, in the car, with relationships, with dependent relatives or money problems can bring us to a point at which we feel trapped and out of control. Before we develop serious health problems we need to slow down and take a good look at the structure of our lives. How much space do we make for ourselves? How much of what we do is really necessary? How can we organise our day to include time to eat three healthy meals in a way that does not ruin our digestion? How can we incorporate three periods of strengthening and revitalising exercise into our week? How can we make sure that each day we will go to bed feeling relaxed and accepting that we spent the day doing as much as we could of what we had to do, but without upsetting our body's equilibrium? Sometimes it is hard to put ourselves first, but little by little we can turn bad habits around and learn to care for our wellbeing and bring a sense of achievement back into our lives.

Aromatic Solutions

Since tension is stored in the muscles of the body, the best way to release that tension is to have a weekly massage. If you do not have a friend or partner who knows how to give a proper massage, try to visit an aromatherapist. A lot of tension can be released by even one massage.

Even so, there is much that you can do for yourself with the aid of some wonderful essential oils. My favourite for releasing tension is myrtle. It is a rubifacient, which means that it brings heat to the area of skin into which it is massaged. Tension can be experienced in various parts of the body: some people may feel that their scalp is too tight, or that their jaw seems to be permanently clenched and tense. However, tension invariably affects the shoulders and base of the neck, and diluted myrtle oil massaged into these areas works wonders. You will experience a pleasantly warm feeling in the muscles, even an hour or so after application; imagine if you will, the heat drawing out the tension from the muscles.

Don't be surprised if you feel a little upset and tearful: this is quite normal when we begin to relax and let go of tension. Sometimes we feel we cannot cope with the pressures of life, and suppress our emotions as we attempt to keep everything together. So before you have a myrtle massage make sure that you have space to let go and plenty of time to give to yourself.

Many essential oils are relaxing, and a simple blend of any of the following can be used to massage the scalp, face or neck (see pages 99 onwards).

Essential oils for Tension

Bergamot
Camomile
Clary sage
Frankincense
Geranium
Lavender
Linden blossom
Marjoram
Neroli
Rose
Rosewood
Sandalwood
Vetivert
Ylang-ylang

Add three drops of one of the oils to 10ml sweet almond oil and massage into the affected area, or make yourself a blend from two or three of the above oils. For example:

10ml sweet almond	*or*	10ml sweet almond
2 drops lavender		1 drop geranium
1 drop marjoram		1 drop frankincense
1 drop neroli *or* bergamot		1 drop ylang-ylang *or* rose

Aromatic baths
Baths containing essential oils are a simple and effective way of releasing tension and a perfect way to end a busy, stressful day. Most of the essential oils listed above are ideal for a bath, but avoid vetivert, sandalwood, linden blossom and rose which are all very thick and difficult to disperse in bath water.

Room fragrancing
Choose an oil from the above list, or make a relaxing blend from two or three different essential oils, and add to the water receptacle of a candle fragrancer. For instance:

1 drop marjoram	*or*	2 drops rosewood
1 drop clary sage		1 drop ylang-ylang
1 drop geranium		

The permutations are endless, and it is not necessary ever to become jaded by a particular fragrance. Be creative.

Other Alternatives

Acupuncture, Bach flower remedies, cranio-sacral therapy, hypnotherapy, NLP, psychotherapy, reflexology, shiatsu.

Thrush

See CANDIDA ALBICANS.

Vomiting

See NAUSEA AND VOMITING.

List of essential oils mentioned in text, along with their Latin names

Angelica	*Angelica archangelica*	Marjoram	
Basil	*Ocimum basilicum*	(Spanish)	*Thymus mastichina*
Bergamot	*Citrus bergamia*	Melissa	*Melissa officinalis*
Black pepper	*Piper nigrum*	Myrtle	*Myrtus communis*
Camomile		Neroli	*Citrus auranthium*
(Roman)	*Anthemis nobilis*		*(flowers)*
Caraway	*Carum carvi*	Niaouli	*Melaleuca viridiflora*
Clary sage	*Salvia sclarea*	Orange	*Citrus auranthium*
Coriander	*Coriandrum sativum*		*(peel)*
Cypress	*Cupressus*	Palmarosa	*Cymbopogon martinii*
	sempivirens	Patchouli	*Pogostemum patchouli*
Eucalyptus	*Eucalyptus globulus*	Peppermint	*Mentha piperita*
Fennel	*Foeniculum vulgare*	Ravansara	*Ravansara aromatica*
Frankincense	*Boswellia carterii*	Rose	*Rosa centifolia/rosa*
Geranium	*Perlargonium*		*damascena*
	graveolens	Rosemary	*Rosmarinus officinalis*
Grapefruit	*Citrus paradisi*	Rosewood	*Aniba parviflora*
Jasmine	*Jasminum officinalis*	Sandalwood	*Santalum album*
Juniper	*Juniperus communis*	Spike	
	(berries)	lavender	*Lavandula latifolia*
Lavender	*Lavandula*	Tea tree	*Melaleuca alternifolia*
	angustifolia	Thyme-linalol	*Thymus vulgaris-*
Lemon	*Citrus limonum*		*linalol*
Lemongrass	*Cymbopogan citratus*	Verbena	*Lippia citriodora*
Linden		Vetivert	*Vetiveria zizanoides*
blossom	*Tilia vulgaris*	Ylang ylang	*Canangium odoratum*

Medical Dictionary

Allopathic Conventional medical treatment which aims to produce a result incompatible with the existing condition. (This is the opposite of homeopathy which treats like with like.)

Angina From the latin angoro to strangle, angina can refer to any disease which is marked by suffocation or constriction. More commonly, it is used for angina pectoris which features a sudden sharp pain in the chest caused by lack of adequate blood supply to the heart.

Antacid A substance which neutralises or counteracts acidity.

Crohns Disease A chronic intestinal disorder in which the segments of the intestine become inflamed and swollen.

Current RDA for Vitamin C – 60mg (Up until recently the RDA was 30mg but an EC directive in 1993 revised this figure.)

DNA Deoxyribonucleic acid, the main constituent of chromosomes, is self-replicating and is responsible for the transmission of hereditary characteristics.

Endocrine System Consists of ductless glands, eg. pituitary, which secrete hormones directly into the blood stream. These hormones are important for metabolic function.

Fibroids A fibromuscular, benign tissue usually found in the uterus.

Free Radicals Exist for a brief period with at least one unpaired electron before reacting to produce a stable molecule.

Gonadotrophin Any hormone which stimulates the ovary or testes.

Hydrogenation The addition of hydrogen to a compound, such as unsaturated fats or fatty acids, which causes soft fats or oils to become saturated.

Leydigs Interstitial Cells Situated in the testes, they are connective tissue cells which secrete the male sex hormone.

Metabolism The series of chemical changes within the body which maintain life through such processes as growth, elimination of waste and production of energy.

Partial Hydrogenation With partial hydrogenation some of the fat content will remain unsaturated.

Pathogen Any agent that causes disease.

Tachycardia Marked increase in the frequency of heart beats.

Bibliography

Which Consumers Guides (1992) (2nd edition) *Understanding Stress*. Consumers Association.

Lewis, D and Stoney, J (1990) *The Doctor's Heart Attack Recovery Plan*. Thorsons.

Nicol, Rosemary (1991) *The Irritable Bowel Stress Book*. Sheldon Press.

Bradley, Dinah (1994) *Hyper-ventilation Syndrome*. Kyle Cathie Ltd.

Booth, Audrey Livingston (1988) *Less Stress, More Success*. Severn House Publishers Ltd.

Macintyre, Anne (1992) (2nd ed.) *ME Post-viral Fatigue Syndrome. How to Live With It*. Unwin Hyman.

Philips, A and Rakusen, J (1989) (2nd ed.) *The New 'Our Bodies, Ourselves.'* Penguin.

Macleod, J (ed) (13th edition) *Davidson's Principles and Practice of Medicine*. Churchill Livingstone.

Houlton, Jane (1993) *The Allergy Survival Guide*. Vermilion, Random House.

De Vries, Jan (1988) *Viruses, Allergies and the Immune System*. Mainstream Publishing Co.

Mumby, Keith (1988) *The Allergy Handbook: A Doctor's Guide to Successful Treatment*. Thorsons.

Wallace, Louise M (1990) *Coping with Angina*. Thorsons.

Stuart, Maryon and Dr Alan Stewart, (1994) *Beat IBS Through Diet*, Vermillion.

Wayne W Topping, PhD (1985) *Stress Release*. Topping Int. Inst. Washington.

Jarvis, DC (MD) (1962) *Arthritis & Folk Medicine*. Pan Books Ltd.

Lewis, Jenny (1993) *The Migraine Handbook.* Vermillion.
Wickett, Jr, MD William (1983) *Herpes: Cause & Control.* Futura Publications, Macdonald & Co (Publishers) Ltd.
Weiner, Michael A, PhD (1986) *Maximum Immunity.* Gateway Books.
Seller, Wanda (1992) *Directory of Essential Oils.* CW Daniel & Co. Ltd.

Recommended Supplements

Biocare
Lakeside, 180 Lifford Lane,
Kings Norton, Birmingham. B30 3NT
Tel: 0121 433 3727
Fax: 0121 433 3879

Solgar
Solgar House, Chiltern Commerce Centre,
Asheridge Road, Chesham, Buck. HP5 2PY

Further Reading

Fats & Oils by Udo Erasmus. Alive Books.

Rose Elliot and Delia Smith are both good authors on the subject of nutrition, and between them offer a range of books.

What Doctors Don't Tell You (WDDTY) is a monthly publication which is highly informative and required reading for anyone who has ever questioned the validity of orthodox medicine.
  Write to; 4 Wallace Road, London N1 2PG

Superbug: Nature's Revenge by Geoffrey Cannon. Virgin Publishing, 1995.

Colour Me Beautiful by Carole Jackson. Piatkus, 1983.

Laughter Is The Best Medicine by Robert W Holden. Thorsons (HarperCollins), 1993.

Rescue Remedy by Gregory Vlamis. Thorsons (Harper Collins), 1994.

Tai Chi Chuan – Meditation in movement featuring Paul Crompton. A Beckmann Communications release.

The Family Guide to Homeopathy by Dr. Andrew Lockie. Elm Tree Books, 1989.

The Complete Homepathy Handbook by Miranda Castro. Macmillan, 1990.

Useful Addresses

Alternative Therapies – Sussex Based

The following practitioners are all known to me personally (as friends as well as therapists) and have each contributed their time and experience to chapter 6 – Alternative Therapies. I make no apologies for the fact that they all live in Sussex, as this county has been my home for more than a decade.

CRANIO-SACRAL THERAPY
Richard Davison MRCST
Craigmore Cottage
Crowborough Hill
Crowborough
E Sussex
TN6 2SE

01892 665492

McTIMONY CHIROPRACTIC
Ruth Urbanowicz BSc., MMCA and Chris Garland MMCA
The Crescent Clinic
37 Vernon Terrace
Brighton
E Sussex
BN1 3JH

01273 202221

NLP (Neuro-linguistic programming)
Gareth Francis BA(Hons), Dip. NLP
Flat 7
19 Preston Park Avenue
Brighton
BN1 6HL

01273 564176

REFLEXOLOGY
Sue Tomkins MIFR
Little Broomham
Broomham Lane
Whitesmith
E Sussex
BN8 6JQ

01825 872277

Sarah Ardern M.Ch.S., B.Sc. (Hons)
The Ardern Foot & Health Clinic
123 St James Street
Brighton
E Sussex
BN2 1TH

01273 673964

HOMEOPATHY
Hanna Waldbaum L.C.H.
Highgate End
Lewes Road
Forest Row
E Sussex
RH18 5AN

01342 823714

HYPNOTHERAPY/PSYCHOTHERAPY
Vincent Tilsley M.A. (Oxon), Dip H.P., M.N.A.H.P.
18 Rosslyn Road,
Shoreham-by-sea
W Sussex
BN43 6WP

01273 463933

ACUPUNCTURE
Marek Urbanowicz M.Ac., M.T.AC.S.
The Crescent Clinic
37 Vernon Terrace
Brighton
E Sussex
BN1 3JH

01273 202221

APPLIED KINESIOLOGY
Marek Urbanowicz M.Ac., M.T.Ac.S. & Member of the
International College of Applied Kinesiology
The Crescent Clinic
37 Vernon Terrace
Brighton
E Sussex
BN1 3JH

01273 202221

SHIATSU
Sarah Bristow M.R.S.S.
The Vinings Clinic
Haywards Heath
W Sussex

01444 417765

BACH FLOWER REMEDIES
Self-treatment is simple and safe.
Nearly every high street health food shop will sell Bach Flower
Remedies and introductory books.
(see Further Reading)

VITAMIN THERAPY
Roberta Morgan Dip I.O.N.
15 London Road
Uckfield
E Sussex
TN22 1JB

01825 767168

Alternative Therapies – National Contact Addresses

Anyone who is not living within easy reach of Sussex may find their local therapist by contacting any of the national organisations as listed below.

CRANIO-SACRAL THERAPY
College of Cranio-Sacral Therapy
160 Upper Fant Road
Maidstone
Kent
ME16 8DJ

01622 729231

McTIMONY CHIROPRACTIC
McTimony Chiropractic Association
21 High Street
Eynsham
Oxford
OX8 1HE

01865 880974

NEURO-LINGUISTIC PROGRAMMING
N.L.P. Association
48 Corser St
Stourbridge
DY8 2DQ

01384 443935

REFLEXOLOGY
International Federation of Reflexologists
78 Eridge Road
Croydon
Surrey
CR0 1EF
0181 667 9458

HOMEOPATHY
The Society of Homeopaths (representing professional homeopaths)
2 Artizan Road
Northampton
NN1 4HU

01604 21400

The British Homeopathic Association (representing medical doctors with additional training in homeopathy)
27A Devonshire Street
London W1N 1RJ
0171 935 2163

BACH FLOWER REMEDIES
Any queries regarding distributors of the Bach Flower Remedies in other parts of the world or for a private consultation, please write to:
Dr Edward Bach Centre
Mount Vernon
Sotwell,
Wallingford
Oxon
OX10 0PZ

VITAMIN THERAPY
Council for Nutrition Education and Therapy (CNEAT)
34 Wadham Road,
London
SW15 2LR

Send £2.00 for CNEAT Directory

Society for the Promotion of Nutritional Therapy
First Floor, The Enterprise Centre
Station Parade
Eastbourne
BN21 1BE

01323 430203

Or ask for details of nutritionists in your area.

SHIATSU
The Shiatsu Society
14 Oakdens Road
Redhill
Surrey
RH1 6BT

HYPNOTHERAPY & PSYCHOTHERAPY
National Association of Counsellors, Hypnotherapists and
Psychotherapists,
Aberystwyth
Dyfed,
Wales
SY23 4EY

01974 241376
or contact:

British Complementary Medicine Association
Admin Office
St Charles Hospital
Exmoor Street
London
W10 6DZ

ACUPUNCTURE
The Council for Acupuncture
179 Gloucester Place
London
NW1 6DX

0171 724 5756

APPLIED KINESIOLOGY
International College of Applied Kineisiology Europe
(ICAKE)
54 East Street
Andover
Hants
SP10 1ES

01264 339 512

Association of Systematic Kinesiology
39 Browns Road
Surbiton
Surrey
KT5 8ST

0181 399 3215
0181 390 1010

Other Alternative Therapies

ARTISTIC THERAPY
There are two distinct trainings in artistic therapy:

1. Jungian
2. Rudolph Steiner

For details of therapists trained in Artistic Therapy based on
anthroposophy (Rudolf Steiner) contact:

Tobias School of Art
Dunnings Road
East Grinstead
W Sussex
RH19 4NF

01342 313655

The Hibernia School of Artistic Therapy,
Hawkwood College
Painswick Old Road
Stroud
Gloucestershire
GL6 7QW

OSTEOPATHY is a manipulative therapy which is widely acclaimed in the treatment of back problems.

ALEXANDER TECHNIQUE works on the principal that when the head is held correctly, the rest of the body will be in alignment and energies are able to flow freely.

HERBAL MEDICINE is a traditional treatment of ailments, both acute and chronic, by the use of medicinal herbs.

CHINESE HERBAL MEDICINE is a traditional Chinese system of treating illness with the use of Chinese herbs used in conjunction with a knowledge of the Chinese five elements.

FLOTATION THERAPY can eliminate stress and worries as the participant floats in a darkened tank of warm water, made bouyant with epsom salts.

Other Useful Addresses

ADD (Attention Deficit Disorder)
Ladder
PO Box 700
Wolverhampton
WV3 7Y

or call the ADD support group on 01373 826045

Essential oils mentioned throughout this book may be obtained by post, along with fragrancers, storage boxes and other books by Maggie Tisserand.
Write to:
Aromatize Products
c/o Maggie Tisserand
8 Paston Place
Brighton
E Sussex
BN2 1HA

Tel: 01273 693622
Fax: 01825 732961

INDEX